THE MEDJUGORJE
PRAYER BOOK

OTHER BOOKS BY WAYNE WEIBLE

Medjugorje: The Message
Letters from Medjugorje
Medjugorje: The Mission
The Final Harvest
A Child Shall Lead Them

the MEDJUGORJE prayer book

POWERFUL PRAYERS FROM THE
APPARITIONS OF THE BLESSED VIRGIN MARY
IN MEDJUGORJE

WAYNE WEIBLE

PARACLETE PRESS
Brewster, Massachusetts

The Medjugorje Prayer Book

2012   Third Printing
2008   Second Printing
2007   First Printing

ISBN: 978-1-55725-530-3

Library of Congress Cataloging-in-Publication Data

Weible, Wayne.
  The Medjugorje prayer book : powerful prayers
from the apparitions of the Blessed Virgin Mary in
Medjugorje / Wayne Weible.
      p. cm.
  ISBN 978-1-55725-530-3
1. Mary, Blessed Virgin, Saint--Prayers and devotions.
2. Mary, Blessed Virgin, Saint--Apparitions and
miracles--Bosnia and Hercegovina--Medugorje. 3.
Catholic Church--Prayers and devotions. 4.
Rosary--Meditations. I. Title.
  BT660.M44W445 2007
  232.91'70949742--dc22   2006102689

10 9 8 7 6 5 4 3

Published by Paraclete Press
Brewster, Massachusetts
www.paracletepress.com
Printed in the United States of America

 *Dedication*

I dedicate this book to the memory of Slavko Barbaric, O.F.M., whose inspiration and leadership in Medjugorje taught us how to pray with the heart.

Contents

ONE

Pray! Pray! Pray!

"Dear children! Also today, I call you to be love where there is hatred and food where there is hunger. Open your hearts, little children, and let your hands be extended and generous so that, through you, every creature may thank God the Creator. Pray, little children, and open your heart to God's love, but you cannot if you do not pray. Therefore, pray, pray, pray. Thank you for having responded to my call."

(Monthly message given September 25, 2004)

She has come to the village of Medjugorje for more than twenty-five years to ask us to pray. She has done so since June 25, 1981, appearing through the mystical power of apparition daily to at least three of an original six children chosen to be visionaries.

She is the Blessed Virgin Mary, mother of Jesus Christ, chosen messenger of God for these times. Her purpose revealed through dramatic messages to the visionaries at Medjugorje is crystal clear: to save her children—all of her children, the washed and the unwashed—through the holy power of prayer.

The Mother of Jesus has made clear that our present-day world is far from the graces of her Son. It is a world without peace. She comes into this caldron of turmoil by God's holy grace calling herself the Queen of Peace. Mary is inviting, urging, pleading, and even begging us to listen, to pray, and to convert our hearts to the ways of Jesus. Because of the positive response by so many, the grace of the Medjugorje message continues.

The apparitions take place in the little township of Medjugorje located in the rugged mountains of Bosnia-Hercegovina, home to the visionaries. The village has become a modern-day Mecca. More than 35 million people have made pilgrimage to the predominantly Croatian Catholic community where they believe the Mother of God is appearing.

People go there for many reasons: curiosity, physical and spiritual healing, desire for solutions to their personal problems, and others. They go to find elusive personal peace. Mostly, though, it is a great place of prayer. Many pilgrims return home spiritually transformed, wanting to do their best to answer the Blessed Virgin's call. Many of them become active graduates of this amazing "School of Prayer."

Two prevalent questions in the hearts of most returning pilgrims—and in the hearts of those who learn of this incredible grace through books, tapes, talks, and personal witness of individuals—are these:

Who is this biblical woman of apparitions?

What does she want from me?

Thus, the purpose of this book is twofold. First, it is to answer these basic questions through learning about the *awesome* power of daily personal and group prayer. Reading Mary's messages given to the world through Medjugorje will help you to understand.

Second, my personal purpose is to give you a guideline for developing an intimate and dynamic prayer life through these lessons. I pray that they will open the hearts of all who read them so that each child of Mary may become an active participant in God's plan of salvation for the world. While the tone of much contained here may sound "Catholic," I mean it for people of all faiths and beliefs.

Using the teaching messages Our Lady has given us at Medjugorje, coupled with my own personal witness, I'll try and give you insight on the above questions as well as the tools needed through my own personal prayers, and much more. I will tell you how she molded my prayer life by her messages to the visionaries at Medjugorje and through personal messages directly and indirectly to me.

Everyone can experience this charism of prayer through intimate guidance by the Blessed Virgin Mary. This is not just for visionaries or unique individuals, but for those who truly believe, surrender to the will of God, and then try to obey the requests of the individual mission given to each of us.

All of us are asked to be participants. But it is our own free will that has to answer yes or no to God's request. In this case, the request comes from Mary in Medjugorje.

To acquire this heavenly grace, it is mandatory to develop an intimacy with our spiritual mother, Mary. This intimacy is necessary to truly accept and develop a strong prayer life with purpose. We begin with our conversations—our prayers—with her and to her. She is affectionately called "Our Lady" or "Blessed Mother" by many who have found that intimacy. These are the names I will refer to or call her in this book as a way of expressing my own intimacy with her.

My qualifications as a writer and commentator on the subject of apparitions of Our Lady and her biblical role are more journalistic and spiritual than they are theological. I am not a priest or minister or theologian. I'm simply a layperson who found spiritual conversion and my own lifetime mission triggered by discovery of this incredible event. But I've been involved in visiting, studying, and investigating the apparitions at Medjugorje for more than twenty years, having traveled there seventy-seven times as of this writing.

I'll tell you of my Medjugorje involvement in the ensuing chapters, but first, let's look at the woman who appears in apparition in Medjugorje. . . .

TWO

Who Is This Woman?

"I am the Blessed Virgin Mary."

". . . I have come because there are many true believers here. I wish to be with you to convert and to reconcile the whole world."

". . . Peace, Peace, Peace! Be reconciled! Only Peace. Make your peace with God among yourselves. For that, it is necessary to believe, to pray, to fast, and to go to confession."

(Messages given June 26, 1981)

Who is this woman of apparitions who comes to teach us through the apparitions in Medjugorje, and why is she the one sent to us in these times? To answer this we need to know a little more about her. There are three critical passages of Scripture that summarize who Mary is, her role in the world today, and her acceptance of that role. I begin with her acceptance of the *first* part of her mission, that of being the human mother, the human *tabernacle* for God to come into the world.

We look in the New Testament to see where Mary's role as messenger for these times originates. In the account in the Gospel of Luke, God sends the Angel Gabriel to greet the teenage Mary. He begins with these words: "Hail, full of grace, the Lord is with you." The salutation is as much title as it is greeting. The powerful archangel asks her to be the mother of the Messiah. She will conceive a child, he tells her, the promised Savior of the world. God Himself will come as a weak, defenseless human baby.

After Mary asks, "How can this be, since I know not a man," the Angel Gabriel tells her not to be afraid, that the Spirit of God will come upon her. She accepts with this humble reply: "I am the handmaid of the Lord. Be it done unto me according to thy word" (Luke 1:26–38).

Thus, Mary is, above all, the human mother of Jesus Christ. In later scriptural passages, she becomes the mother given to us as a *spiritual mother*, the *second* part of her mission, directly from the cross by her Son.

Can you imagine Jesus suffering from more than five thousand inflicted wounds, cruelly nailed to a cross to die an excruciating death of suffocation, pushing up on torn, bloodied feet, to say in agonizing short breaths: "Woman, behold thy son!" and to John, the beloved disciple, standing in for us: "Son, behold thy mother!" (John 19:25–27)? Can we really see this as a Jewish son telling a friend to take care of his mom now that he will be gone?

I find it difficult to look at this dramatic horror as simply an act by a loving son to make sure that his mother would be taken care of domestically after his death. It is Jesus, the Man-God, giving His mother the second part of her mission: to lead us to Him, to His gift of salvation through death on the cross.

This is Mary, the chosen mother of Christ and the appointed spiritual mother, who is fulfilling her mission through the apparitions in Medjugorje. She has done this in past apparitions as well, notably in La Salette (France, 1846), Lourdes (France, 1858), and primarily in Fatima (Portugal, 1917). If you do not know about past apparitions of the Blessed Virgin—including her appearance to

Catherine Labouré at Rue du Bac, Paris, France, 1830, and as early as 1531 in Guadalupe, Mexico—you may want to learn about them to fully understand the magnitude of the Medjugorje apparitions. Historical understanding will help you see the unifying scope of the great gift of grace God has given us through all of Mary's apparitions.

Next, we skip ahead to Mary's mission and how it plays out in these modern times—and, as many, including myself, believe, the end times of this era of unsettled peace. Mary is described in the Book of Revelation as ". . . a woman clothed with the sun, the moon under her feet and on her head a crown of twelve stars" (12:1). This is the woman who appears in Medjugorje. According to the visionaries' descriptions, she has a crown of twelve stars on her head and, each time she appears, she comes in a brilliance of light—literally clothed with the sun. She makes it abundantly clear in her numerous messages that she comes now to prepare us for these *final* times before her Son brings His peace that passes all understanding to earth. She even stated to the visionaries in an early message that ". . . *These will be my last apparitions on earth.*" Mary tells us this blunt truth, but mercifully adds, ". . . *because it will no longer be necessary.*"

The reason that future apparitions will no longer be necessary is that the mission God gave her will be complete. Shortly after the end of her appearances to the last visionary, the special future-events messages, or secrets, as we call them, will begin to occur. At their conclusion, the peace of Jesus Christ will reign on earth again, and the children of God will worship Him as they did in ancient times.

This is the same "Gospa" (the literal translation for "Our Lady" in the Croatian language she uses to speak to her visionaries in Medjugorje) quoted in the Scriptures above. She is fulfilling Holy Scripture, giving us affirming messages of learning and hope, and she does so with a motherly, hands-on approach.

As if to confirm her mission in these modern times, Our Lady began her conversation to the visionaries on June 25, 1981, with these words: *"Praise be Jesus!"* She still greets the visionaries this way with each apparition. We can know *almost certainly* that heaven sends the entity that appears to the visionaries in Medjugorje, because Satan cannot utter these words! She follows them with this statement from her first conversation with the visionaries: *"I am the Blessed Virgin Mary, and I have come to tell you that God exists and that He loves you!"*

Thus, Mary gives immediate confirmation in Medjugorje as to who she is and who sent her. When the visionaries asked her why she was appearing in their village, she replied, *"I have come because there are many true believers here. I wish to be with you to convert and to reconcile the whole world."* This message, along with the greeting, gives full context to her mission for these times.

I hope that you now have a clearer idea of who this lady of apparitions is and why she is the one sent from heaven as messenger for these times. Possibly from the Scripture passages and her first messages, you can see her overall intent in desiring to bring *all of us*, her children, to her Son through a stronger prayer life. There's a lot more "evidence" through her words to the visionaries, and we'll cover it in the ensuing pages.

Let me point out one more overriding trait of Mary that I have discovered in my years of involvement in the Medjugorje apparitions. Statues, paintings, icons, and other images consistently portray the Blessed Virgin Mary as somber, pious, unsmiling, solemn, and grave. From the beginning of my experiences with her, she is seen and heard as a breathtakingly beautiful, graciously informal, and, above all, intimate Mary. I am left with this feeling in prayer and thought. Intimacy is the same feeling described by the visionaries after each encounter with Our Lady. This is her way of reassuring us that she is indeed the spiritual mother of the world.

We begin our experience of the power of prayer through the Medjugorje apparitions with Mary's basic message to us, made clear from the first day:

Pray! Pray! Pray!

THREE

Her Teachings in the "School of Prayer"

"Dear children, I have chosen this parish in a special way, and I wish to lead it. I am guarding it in love and I want everyone to be mine. Thank you for having responded tonight. I wish you always to be with me and my Son in ever greater numbers. I shall give a message to you every Thursday."

(Message given March 1, 1984)

As if to underline the urgency of our times, Mary has been giving teaching messages meant for each one of us through the visionaries, daily, weekly, and monthly. During the first thirty-three months, the Blessed Mother taught the visionaries, the villagers, and the children of the world in her special Medjugorje "School of Prayer."

At first, the "Teacher" came daily in a brilliance of three flashes of strange light, radiating joy and singular beauty, gaining our attention by interceding for us with a spectacular spiritual show of miracles and healings. Mary introduced basic spiritual tools—prayer, fasting, and penance—that those in Medjugorje would have to learn and use properly if the apparitions were to succeed. And indeed, its success very much depended on the reception of her students. They would be required to learn and to practice what they learned by words and actions, and to share it with others: their neighbors, at first, and later, the waves of pilgrims that would begin to come.

These were the kindergarten and lower grades of the School of Prayer. Mary's teaching worked so well that the visionaries and villagers soon moved into the upper grades!

Mary began teaching with the message given on March 1, 1984, that she presented to the parish through the visionary Marija. On Thursday of that week she began, *"Thank you for having responded to my call, dear children, for you in the parish to be converted. This is my wish. That way all who come here shall be able to convert!"* This marked the

start of a weekly mission initiated by Mary to
personally teach the people of the village.

The weekly teachings by Mary to the
parish continued the following week—
*"Dear children, in a special way this evening
I am calling you during Lent to honor the
wounds of my Son, which He received from
the sins of this parish. Unite yourselves with
my prayers for the parish that His sufferings
may be bearable. Thank you for having
responded to my call."*

March 29: *"Dear children, in a special way
this evening I am calling on you to have per-
severance in times of trial. Consider how the
Almighty is still suffering today on account of
your sins. So when sufferings come, offer
them up as a sacrifice to God. Thank you for
having responded to my call."*

April 5: *"Dear children, this evening I pray
you especially to venerate the Heart of my
Son, Jesus. Make reparation for the wound
inflicted on the Heart of my Son. That Heart
is offended by all kinds of sins. Thank you for
coming this evening."*

April 12: *"Dear children, today I beseech
you to stop slandering and to pray for the unity
of the parish, because my Son and I have a*

*special plan for this parish. Thank you for
having responded to my call."*

April 19 (Holy Thursday): *"Dear children,
sympathize with me! Pray, pray, pray!"*

And then, a startling pause interrupted the
teachings. After almost two months of weekly
messages, attendance at St. James Church on
Thursday evenings unbelievably had plummeted
from standing room only to just half full. What
had been a spectacular and dramatic event had
quickly developed into a routine thing for
many of the faithful. On Thursday, April 26,
Marija prayed and waited; the people of the
village waited. No apparition—no teaching
message.

The people left the church disappointed and
confused. Marija was also confused but said
nothing about it over the following three days.
On Monday, Marija finally asked, "Dear
Madonna, why didn't you give me a message
for the parish on Thursday?" Our Lady
responded: *"I do not wish to force anyone to
do that which he or she neither feels nor
desires, even though I had special messages for
the parish by which I wanted to awaken the
faith of every believer. But only a really small
number has accepted my Thursday messages.*

In the beginning there were quite a few. But it's become a routine affair for them. And now recently some are asking for the message out of curiosity, and not out of faith and devotion to my Son and me."

This last message shook people, and most realized what a special grace they had been given. It was like getting a D on a test! Our Lady did not appear or speak the next week, but on Thursday, May 10, she did—to a packed house. She said, *"I am speaking to you and I wish to speak on. You just listen to my instructions!"* With that, order was restored to the classroom! In addition, there was forgiveness by the teacher. On May 17, she gave this message: *"Dear children, today I am very happy because there are many who want to consecrate themselves to me. Thank you. You have not made a mistake. My Son, Jesus Christ, wishes to bestow on you special graces through me. My Son is happy because of your dedication. Thank you for having responded to my call."*

The weekly Thursday evening messages would go on for a little more than two and a half years. Can you imagine? Here is the Blessed Virgin Mary, not only choosing their parish as an apparition site, not only choosing six of their young people to be visionaries and messengers to the world, but now giving weekly lessons of grace!

Graduation from the upper grades of the School of Prayer brought the villagers to a new level of understanding. This was a level that would include the entire world, truly anyone who would listen and try to live what she was teaching them. On January 7, 1987, Mary gave this message to Marija for the villagers: *"Dear children, I want to thank you for your response to my messages, especially, dear children, thank you for all the suffering and prayers you have offered to me. Dear children, I want to give you messages from now on no longer every Thursday, but on the 25th of each month. The time has come when what my Lord wanted has been fulfilled. From now on, I will give you fewer messages; but I will be with you. Dear children, I beg you listen to my messages and to live them so that I can guide you. Thank you for having responded to my call."*

Then came the first of the monthly messages, on January 25, 1987: *"Dear children, behold, also today I want to call you to start living a new life as of today. Dear children, I want you to comprehend that God has chosen each one of you, in order to use you in a great plan for the salvation of mankind. You are not able to comprehend how great your role is in God's design. Therefore, dear children, pray so that in prayer you may be able to comprehend what God's plan is in your regard. I am with you in order that you may be able to bring it about in all its fullness. Thank you for having responded to my call."*

All in the village could see that the first phase of this wondrous gift was completed, and they were moving on to a higher plane, one that would include every place in the world outside of their village.

The overall tone of the messages changed noticeably. They were longer and more detailed, and strongly emphasized prayer above all, like this one given April 25: *"Dear children, today also I am calling you to prayer. You know, dear children, that God grants special graces in prayer. Therefore, seek and pray in order that you may be able to comprehend all that I am giving here. I call you, dear children, to prayer with the heart. You know that without prayer you cannot comprehend all that God is planning through each one of you. Therefore, pray! I desire that through each one of you God's plan may be fulfilled, that all which God has planted in your heart may keep on growing. So pray that God's blessing may protect each one of you from all the evil that is threatening you. I bless you, dear children. Thank you for having responded to my call."*

The same emphasis is evident in the ensuing months and even years, as seen in these examples:

February 25, 1988: *"Dear children, today again I am calling you to prayer and complete surrender to God. You know that I love you and am coming here out of love, so I could show you the path of peace and salvation for your souls. I want you to obey me and not permit Satan to seduce you. Dear children, Satan is very strong and, therefore, I ask you to dedicate your prayers to me so that those who are under his influence may be saved. Give witness by your life, sacrifice your lives for the salvation of the world. I am with you and I am grateful to you, but in heaven you shall receive the Father's reward which He has promised you. Therefore, little children, do not be afraid. If you pray, Satan cannot injure you even a little, because you are God's children and He is watching over you. Pray, and let the Rosary always be in your hands as a sign to Satan that you belong to me. Thank you for having responded to my call."*

February 25, 1989: *"Dear children, today I am calling you to prayer of the heart. Throughout this season of grace, I desire each of you to be united with Jesus; but without unceasing prayer, you cannot experience the beauty and greatness of the grace which God is offering you. Therefore, little children, at all times fill your heart with even the smallest prayers. I am with you and unceasingly I keep watch over every heart which is given to me. Thank you for having responded to my call."*

November 25, 1989: *"Dear children, I have been inviting you for years by these messages which I am giving you. Little children, by means of the messages, I wish to make a very beautiful mosaic in your heart so I may be able to present each one of you to God like the original image. Therefore, little children, I desire that your decisions be free before God, because He has given you freedom. Therefore, pray so that, free from any influence of Satan, you may decide only for God. I am praying for you before God, and I am seeking your surrender to God. Thank you for having responded to my call."*

As you see, a gentle but urgent call to those whom Mary wishes to become children of God fills each monthly message. She calls us *especially* through prayer. She calls us especially who are so openly exposed to the influence of Satan, who wants nothing more than to take away all that she has come to give us.

You may be asking yourself why we are so graced to be living in a time when the Mother of God comes to earth to speak to each of us so personally and so intimately.

In other words, why me?

Why Has She Chosen Me?

"Dear children, today I want to wrap you all in my mantle and lead you all along the way of conversion. Dear children, I beseech you, surrender to the Lord your entire past, all the evil that has accumulated in your hearts. I want each one of you to be happy. Therefore, dear children, pray, and in prayer you shall realize a new way of joy. Joy will manifest in your hearts and thus you shall be joyful witness of that which I and My Son want from each one of you. I am blessing you. Thank you for having responded to my call."

(Monthly message given February 25, 1987)

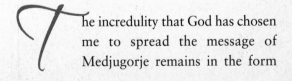

he incredulity that God has chosen me to spread the message of Medjugorje remains in the form of a permanent question seared into my mind. It is a question I ask every day: Why me?

My own conversion to a mission of spreading the Medjugorje messages began with a shocking and soul-shaking personal miracle— that of *literally* hearing Our Lady speaking directly to my heart. I include an account of that miracle in this book.

Mary has spoken to my heart many times since that first occasion. Sometimes she speaks directly to me and, at other times, through visionaries or inner locutionaries or other individuals. I know now that these messages are gifts given to us by the Holy Spirit when we truly begin a process of surrending our souls to Jesus. They are not given just to "holy" souls. Our Lady made that clear from the first week of the apparitions in Medjugorje when the visionary Mirjana asked Our Lady why she had chosen them. "Why are you appearing to us? We are no better than others." She replied with a smile and said, *"I do not necessarily choose the best."* I can strongly relate to that!

Before learning about Medjugorje, I was a lukewarm soul, a Lutheran Protestant, one who didn't care too much for Catholics.

Martin Luther and his followers had "reformed" the church, gotten it right after 1,500 years of its existence. The church was corrupt and Lutherans had cleaned it up. That's what I was taught.

I first heard about Medjugorje during a Sunday school class I was teaching at my Lutheran church in October 1985. To be honest, I had no business teaching such a class and was doing so only because I thought it might help me socially. In addition, it might be good for a few business contacts. I asked so many questions that they asked me to teach. My ego wouldn't let me say no. I had only returned to going to church less than two years before after seven years of no church in my life, having walked away in anger because of a divorce following fourteen years of marriage.

I really didn't know much about Scripture and usually did anything I could to avoid getting into deep discussions about the Bible, even though every lesson plan was based on gospel teachings. I would often come up with my own lesson plans, which is why on this particular Sunday we were animatedly discussing modern-day miracles.

As the class was coming to a close, one of the woman members said, "Speaking of miracles, let me tell you what one of my Catholic friends recently told me. There's this little village in Yugoslavia where six kids are saying that the Blessed Virgin Mary has been appearing to them and speaking to them, and that it has been going on daily for over four years." She then sat back with a smug, can-you-top-that smile.

My knee-jerk reaction was, what nonsense! How could this Mary be appearing? She lived, she died, and that was the end of that. Besides, everyone knows she's Catholic—or, at least anything to do with the Blessed Virgin people view as Catholic. As a newspaper journalist who owned and published four weekly community newspapers and who was trained to be a skeptic of anything that could not be authenticated or proven, I immediately rejected the story, personally and professionally.

Yet, there was a curiosity. My business sense picked up the scent of a possible story. Christmas was not too far away, and this might be interesting subject matter for the holiday season. I asked the woman if she could give me more details, maybe a book or other source of research on the apparitions. Yes, she said, her friend had a videotape recently made during the time of an actual apparition at Medjugorje, and she was sure she could borrow it for me.

Several days later I viewed the videotape. With pencil and paper at hand to make notes, I watched and listened with skepticism well in the forefront of my mind. Ten minutes later, I had not made one note. I was totally mesmerized by what I was seeing and hearing!

Halfway through the tape, made four years after the start of the apparitions, I watched the young visionaries as they prepared for the daily apparition with the praying of the Rosary. As I viewed the up-close scan of the visionaries' faces, I suddenly thought, I believe this! With that realization I felt a wave of guilt. If this was real, then God was real. I believed before, but never really believed beyond a distant thought that God might be real. If He were real, He knew everything about me.

And then the miracle that would transform my life occurred. The guilt vanished as quickly as it had come and I had a sense of great peace. All at once, this same Virgin Mary—

this "Catholic" Mary—was speaking to me! Not in actual audible words but very clearly within my heart, she said, *"You are my son and I am asking you to do my Son's will."*

I fell back into my chair, stunned and in physical shock. How could this be? I wasn't Catholic! I wasn't even a good Christian! Yet, her message continued: *"I am asking you to spread the messages I am giving here and if you choose, the spreading of these messages will become your life's mission."*

There was no denying the reality of what was happening. I had no idea of why I was the one asked to do this, but finally, I mentally mumbled a weak, "I'll try. . . ."

In the weeks that followed this incredible personal miracle, I learned that a simple, weak yes is all Our Lady needs from us. Once we commit, once we allow her just a little crack of space into our hearts and minds, she takes care of the rest.

Within a year, everything in my life had changed. By April 1986, I had sold my businesses and was making plans to go to Medjugorje. Less than a month later, on May 1 of that same year, I arrived in the little village, unaware of the significance of that day as a special Marian feast day. I returned in June and again in November.

In those trips, the Blessed Virgin Mary became my constant guide, with more miracles and personal words to my heart. I actually began writing my first book, *Medjugorje: The Message,* at the foot of the huge cement cross on top of the mountain that overlooks the valley. I did so because I felt she was asking me to begin it there. In the ensuing years, I have come to expect nothing less from her. She is my "everything" when it comes to my spiritual life and mission.

Since that miraculous day, Mary has sent me to nearly every major city and town in the United States and to hundreds of smaller places, including dozens of countries throughout the world. I've spoken in thousands of Catholic and non-Catholic churches, bringing the messages of prayer, fasting, and penance given at Medjugorje to millions of us.

That first book, *Medjugorje: The Message,* written nearly twenty years ago, has reached over a million copies sold and is still going strong. This is all the work of the Holy Spirit. Only through the Holy Spirit can Mary come in apparition, or speak or appear to anyone.

Our Lady could have chosen any person and asked him or her to take on this particular mission. As Mother Angelica of EWTN Television fame said to me when I appeared on her show in 1988, still a Protestant at the time, "God can choose any dummy off the street and make them an instrument of His message!" She then quickly caught herself and said, "Oh, I didn't mean to call you a dummy!" but it was too late; the audience roared with laughter. Truth be known, though, she was right!

All of the graces of God come through the Holy Spirit. Without that grace, I would not have been part of the Medjugorje miracle.

Let's take a look at that holy power and how it works.

FIVE

We Begin with Holy Power

". . . With prayer and fasting, one can stop wars; one can alter the laws of nature."

(Message given July 1982)

*T*he holy power of prayer comes from invoking the presence of the Holy Spirit. Our Lady asks us to begin all of our prayers with a prayer to the Holy Spirit and to end all of our prayers with a prayer to the Holy Spirit.

We can see the potential of this holy power in the message above, where she states simply but profoundly that with prayer and fasting, we can stop wars and we can alter the laws of nature. She is teaching us that with prayer and fasting, we can stop actual wars between nations; we can stop wars between religions;

we can stop wars between families and family members; and, most important, we can stop the war that rages inside of each of us between good and evil.

Let's be clear about fasting and penance. They are an extension and/or form of prayer, and when they are used in conjunction with invocations of prayer, you have the equivalent of nuclear holy power!

So how does this holy power work? Perhaps the following parable will make it easier to understand:

There was a man who lived alone at the top of a very high mountain. A devout man who loved God deeply, he had chosen to live life as a religious hermit. Prayer was his main mission. He relied on prayer for everything and strongly believed that God was listening and reacting positively to every word.

Each Friday the hermit would make his way down the mountain in an ancient vehicle to buy provisions for the week. He found it a difficult trip, with just enough room on the narrow, winding road to cautiously maneuver his way to the small village in the valley below.

One Friday, following a night wracked with violent rains and howling winds, the hermit started on his weekly trip only to be stopped halfway down by a large boulder that had fallen onto the road during the storm and completely blocked the way. There was not even enough room to squeeze by on foot.

The hermit returned to his home and began praying, asking God to remove the stone from the road, convinced that by the next morning, the stone would be gone.

But it wasn't.

Puzzled, the hermit returned to his home and again prayed without ceasing. "Lord, didn't you hear me praying yesterday?" he said plaintively. "I asked You to move the stone so that I can get to the valley for supplies." Surely God would respond and move the stone.

Yet again the next day the stone still blocked the road.

With no other choice, the hermit returned to his home. He began to ration his supplies and prayed with even greater fervor; still, the stone remained, blocking the road.

By the sixth day, the hermit was desperate. Supplies were dwindling. The stone was still there in the road. Maybe, he thought, if he tried to push the stone, the Lord would give him immediate strength to move it. So he began pushing with all his might.

The stone didn't move. Day after day, he pushed against the stone to no avail.

Two weeks later, having pushed on the stone daily, and now with only a few days of rationed supplies left, he once again approached the stone and began pushing. Suddenly, the stone moved slightly. Excitedly, the hermit pushed and pushed, with the stone moving a little each time. Several days later, with a mighty heave by the hermit, the stone tumbled over the side of the road, at last clearing a way to the valley for supplies.

That evening, after a wonderful meal and filled with contentment, the hermit prayed in joy, thanking God for removing the stone. That night, as he prepared for bed, he noticed his reflection in the mirror. He was surprised, because he looked different. His muscles were larger and his entire body was transformed into that of a fine athlete. He was amazed!

Suddenly, the hermit realized what had happened. Days of pushing against the stone had caused the physical change in his body. As he got stronger, he was finally able to move the stone. God had heard his prayers and God had responded. God had done so in a very revealing way: He had given the hermit the tools through his strengthened body to answer his own prayer for removal of the stone!

The moral of the story is obvious: when we empower the Holy Spirit in our prayer and fasting and penance, we use our own spiritual strengths to answer our own prayer requests! The Holy Spirit is the provider of spiritual strength, a unique source of divine power. Our Lady confirmed this in an early message on June 3, 1983, when she said (referring to a question about the Holy Spirit): "He only has one nature, the Divine nature." In the same message she replied this way when the visionaries asked if Father Tomislav Vlasic (who was the pastor of St. James at that time) should ask the parish to fast and pray in hopes that the Church would recognize the supernatural events taking place in Medjugorje: *"Yes it is a good way. Have the parish pray for this gift. Have them pray also for the gift of the Holy Spirit so that all those who come here will feel the presence of God."*

Mary's early weekly messages given to the visionaries in Medjugorje also reinforce what I am saying here about holy power:

Weekly message of November 8, 1984: *"Dear children, you are not conscious of the messages which God is sending you through me. He is giving you great graces and you do not comprehend them. Pray to the Holy Spirit for enlightenment. If you only knew how great are the graces God is granting you, you would be praying ceaselessly."*

Weekly message of April 11, 1985: *"Dear children, today I wish to say to everyone in the parish to pray in a special way to the Holy Spirit for enlightenment. From today God wishes to test the parish in a special way in order that He might strengthen it in faith."*

Weekly message of May 9, 1985: *"Dear children, no, you do not know how many graces God is giving you. You do not want to move ahead during these days when the Holy Spirit is working in a special way. Your hearts are turned toward the things of earth and they preoccupy you. Turn your hearts toward prayer and seek the Holy Spirit to be poured out on you."*

Now, let's put the holy power of prayer to work. We begin with special prayers to the Holy Spirit. . . .

SIX

Come, Holy Spirit!

"Dear children! Also today I call you to prayer. Renew your personal prayer, and in a special way pray to the Holy Spirit to help you pray with the heart. I intercede for all of you, little children, and call all of you to conversion. If you convert, all those around you will also be renewed and prayer will be a joy for them. Thank you for having responded to my call."

(Monthly message given May 25, 2003)

So now we actually begin looking at the prayers that Our Lady gives us. Because of her messages, I know to begin all prayers and prayer sessions, individually and in groups, with a prayer to the Holy Spirit. I know to pray expressly for the intentions within my heart. I know to pray with purpose and to explain in detail those intentions. That is what Our Lady has taught me and reinforced in my heart.

Here is a highly recommended prayer to begin all of our prayers:

Come, Holy Spirit, come through the intercession of the Immaculate Heart of Mary, your beloved Spouse.

If you want to personalize the prayer, you can add such things as "the Immaculate Heart of Mary of Medjugorje," or transform it in other ways. Remember, prayer is a conversation with God that doesn't have to contain *thees* and *thous* and *thys* to be effective.

You can also use this special prayer to the Holy Spirit that I feel Our Lady gave me and asked me to use daily. I usually pray this at the start of the day:

Come, Holy Spirit, enlighten my heart to the ways of God;
Come, Holy Spirit, into my mind so that I know the things that are of God;

Come, Holy Spirit, into my very soul so
that I belong entirely to God;
Sanctify every thought, word, and deed,
so that all will be for the glory of God.

There are other special prayers to the Holy
Spirit that many of us use, such as these:

Send forth your Spirit, O Lord, and renew
the face of the earth.

❧

Come, Holy Spirit; come, divine power of
love, come and fill my poor heart: purify
it, sanctify it, and make it all Yours.

❧

Holy Spirit, I want to do what is right;
Help me.
Holy Spirit, I want to live like Jesus;
Guide me.
Holy Spirit, I want to pray like Jesus;
Teach me.

With these invocations to the Holy Spirit,
we begin our actual application of prayer, of
conversation with God, gleaned from the
information and teachings of Mary's messages
at Medjugorje.

SEVEN

Pray My Rosary!

"Dear children, today, like never before, I invite you to prayer. Your prayer should be a prayer for peace. Satan is strong and wishes not only to destroy human life, but also nature and the planet on which we live. Therefore, dear children, pray that you can protect yourselves, through prayer, with the blessing of God's peace. God sends me to you so that I can help you if you wish to accept the rosary. Even the rosary alone can work miracles in the world and in your lives. I bless you and I stay among you as long as it is God's will. Thank you for not betraying my presence here, and I thank you because your response is serving God and peace. Thank you for having responded to my call."

(Monthly message given January 25, 1991)

verything Mary has said about prayer to this point is employed in her Holy Rosary prayers. Just as prayer is the foundation of the Medjugorje messages, the powerful Rosary is the foundation prayer of our daily prayer life. I discovered that early in my mission.

Shortly after Our Lady spoke to my heart that first time in October 1985, I was given a rosary. I had just run the first of what would become a series of articles about the apparitions in my newspapers. A nun telephoned my office and asked me to come to the local Catholic church so that she could give me a present for running the articles. She simply could not get over the idea that a Lutheran Protestant—and a journalist to boot—was writing about apparitions of the Blessed Virgin Mary. She wanted to show her appreciation.

She gave me a rosary with a little booklet explaining how to pray it. I paid no attention to the booklet, looked at the rosary, and said to her, "Thank you, that's a lovely necklace and my wife will love it!" She laughed and told me that it wasn't necessarily a necklace, although I could use it as such, but that it was a special prayer of the Blessed Virgin Mary. The booklet would explain how to pray it.

Grateful for her response but really untouched by the idea of it as a prayer, I took it home, placed it on my bedside table, and forgot about it. Actually, I did remember once seeing a movie where someone was praying with a string of beads. All I recalled from the film were the words, "Hail Mary, blessed are you . . ." So I would say this phrase while running on the beach, which I did almost every day. I was constantly aware of Mary after her message to me and thought a lot about her, but had never attempted any kind of prayer to her other than this little phrase. That became my first attempt to pray to her.

On January 1, 1986, New Year's Day, I noticed the rosary again and thought about praying it. I noticed it because I was sick in bed with the flu. Very sick! So sick that I thought I'd better at least look at the little book, try to follow its directions and pray this Rosary prayer that Our Lady seemed to love so much.

On finishing my first Rosary, I felt a sense of peace beyond explanation and stated out loud to God (not to the Blessed Virgin Mary),

"Lord, I'm going to pray this Rosary every day for the rest of my life." I have done so every day since, having prayed thousands of Rosaries. The wonder is that each time I pray it, it is different; it is never repetitive or boring. Without this wonderful prayer, neither my mission nor my conversion would have been complete.

Each bead of each Rosary prayed can or should be for a special intention or person. This applies first and foremost to family concerns, giving grace and purpose to prayer. All prayers, but the Rosary especially, should be prayed in what I call "freefall," that is, timelessness. In other words, we shouldn't worry about the time it takes to pray; we just pray with no sense of time. I've prayed Rosaries in as little as ten minutes and as much as forty minutes. I've participated in group Rosaries— led by priests, no less—that they prayed in less than ten minutes!

Rosaries can be prayed with general or specific meditations—that is, the entire prayer for a single or general intention—or specific intentions with each bead and/or each decade. The point is, make each part of the Rosary prayer count!

I relate to you now the prayers I feel Our Lady has placed in my heart. There are two forms of the Rosary I pray and recommend to all. The first one contains short, informal meditations before each decade. The second form is a more formal meditation before each decade, based on words received directly from Jesus. I have found this a powerful, meditative Rosary structure that a locutionist named Patsy Soto taught me. There is more about this in the chapter on formal meditations.

First, let's look at the informal meditations. I begin with the assumption that you, the reader, know how to pray the Rosary. However, I have listed the prayers of the Creed, Our Father, Hail Mary, and O My Jesus in the opening mysteries in case you are not familiar with them.

EIGHT

My Informal Meditations of the Rosary

"I ask only to pray with fervor. Prayer must become a part of your daily life to permit the true faith to take root."

(Message given September 8, 1981)

OPENING LINES

All praise, glory and honor to You, Lord Jesus Christ. You are the King of eternal glory!

✤

Come, Holy Spirit, fill our hearts with Your presence as we pray the Holy Rosary.

✤

We pray for all of Our Lady's intentions and _____ (here you may add your personal intentions; again, I remind you to personalize your prayers so that they remain earnest, specific, and personal).

In Medjugorje, the full Rosary is prayed in the evening, starting at 5:00 PM in the winter months and 6:00 PM during the summer. The Rosary begins with the Apostles' Creed and then goes directly into the mysteries, skipping the Our Father, the three Hail Marys, and the Glory Be that normally precede the four mysteries. I pray a portion of the Divine Mercy prayers as my entry into the mysteries and list it following the Creed.

THE CREED

I believe in God, the Father Almighty, Creator of heaven and earth, and in Jesus Christ, His only Son, our Lord, who was conceived by the Holy Spirit, born of the Virgin Mary, suffered under Pontius Pilate, was crucified, died, and was buried. He descended into hell. The third day He arose again from the dead. He ascended into heaven and is seated at the right hand of the Father. From thence He shall come to judge the living and the dead.

I believe in the Holy Spirit, the holy catholic church, the communion of saints, the forgiveness of sins, the resurrection of the body, and the life everlasting. Amen.

For my personal entry into the mysteries, which takes the place of the traditional Our Father, three Hail Marys, and the Glory Be, I use a prayer from the Divine Mercy prayers. As noted earlier, the Medjugorje Rosary prayer begins with the Creed and then continues right into the mysteries. The purpose of the entry prayer is to put us in the proper frame of mind to pray.

MY ENTRY PRAYER

Eternal Father, I offer You the body, blood, soul, and divinity of our dearly beloved Lord, Jesus Christ, in atonement for our sins and those of the whole world. For the sake of His sorrowful passion, have mercy on us and on the whole world.

The Joyful Mysteries
OF THE HOLY ROSARY

The First Joyful Mystery:
The Annunciation

MY INFORMAL MEDITATION

Dear Mother, let us say as you did, "Let it be done to me according to your word. . . ." Help us to open ourselves in humility and love to the call of your Son, Jesus.

OUR FATHER

Our Father, who is in heaven, hallowed be Your name. Your kingdom come, Your will be done, on earth as it is in heaven.

Give us this day our daily bread, and forgive us our trespasses as we forgive those who trespass against us; and lead us not into temptation, but deliver us from evil. Amen.

HAIL MARY
(ten times)

Hail Mary, full of grace, the Lord is with you. Blessed are you among women, and blessed is the fruit of your womb, Jesus.

Holy Mary, Mother of God, pray for us sinners, now and at the hour of our death. Amen.

GLORY BE

Glory be to the Father, the Son, and the Holy Spirit; as it was in the beginning, is now, and always will be, world without end. Amen.

O MY JESUS

O my Jesus, forgive us our sins; save us from the fires of hell. Lead all souls to heaven, and help especially those who are in need of Your mercy. Amen.

⁂

The Second Joyful Mystery: The Visit to Elizabeth

This mystery is my absolute favorite of all the mysteries of the Holy Rosary. It is Elizabeth's response to Mary's visit: "Who am I that the mother of my Lord should come to me?"—a question I still ask daily.

INFORMAL MEDITATION

Holy Mary, who am I that you should come to me? Thank you for coming to Medjugorje. Help me to answer your call with humility and love.

OUR FATHER ✳ HAIL MARY 10X ✳ GLORY BE ✳
O MY JESUS

❦

The Third Joyful Mystery:
The Birth of Jesus

INFORMAL MEDITATION

Jesus, You have come into the world as a helpless baby, to live as we live, to work as we work, and then to die a horrible death on the cross so that we may have eternal salvation. Thank you, Jesus, for Your life and for Your death.

OUR FATHER ✳ HAIL MARY 10X ✳ GLORY BE ✳
O MY JESUS

❦

The Fourth Joyful Mystery:
The Presentation

INFORMAL MEDITATION

Holy Mother of Jesus, we ask you to intercede for all priests and religious so that they may know that He is the promised Savior.

OUR FATHER ✳ HAIL MARY 10X ✳ GLORY BE ✳
O MY JESUS

❦

The Fifth Joyful Mystery:
Finding the Child Jesus in the Temple

INFORMAL MEDITATION

Dearest Mary, as we think of the child Jesus found in the temple, we pray for all children of all ages throughout the world to be guided by heaven and assisted by us.

OUR FATHER ✳ HAIL MARY 10X ✳ GLORY BE ✳
O MY JESUS

Hail holy Queen, Mother of mercy, our life, our sweetness, and our hope! To thee do we cry, poor banished children of Eve. To thee do we send up our sighs, mourning and weeping in this vale of tears.

Turn, then, most gracious advocate, thine eyes of mercy toward us, and after this our exile show unto us the blessed fruit of thy womb, Jesus. O clement, O loving, O sweet Virgin Mary.

❦

I have placed the recently added Mysteries of Illumination of the Holy Rosary, added by Pope John Paul II, in this order of praying the Rosary because it fits chronologically. While we can pray these at any time, these more recent mysteries allow for a proper flow to the prayer in meditating on the life of Jesus.

The Mysteries of Illumination
OF THE HOLY ROSARY

(You may pray separately and begin with the standard entry prayers or with your own personal entry prayers.)

The First Mystery of Illumination:
The Baptism of Jesus

INFORMAL MEDITATION

Lord, may we renew our own baptism vows as we contemplate Your example by being baptized by your precursor, John the Baptist.

OUR FATHER ✳ HAIL MARY 10X ✳ GLORY BE ✳
O MY JESUS

❦

The Second Mystery of Illumination:
The Miracle at the Wedding Feast of Cana

INFORMAL MEDITATION

Jesus, You perform Your first miracle for Your mother and begin Your public ministry. Dearest Mother, may we respond to your call to the wine servants as you tell them to "Do as He tells you."

OUR FATHER ✳ HAIL MARY 10X ✳ GLORY BE ✳

O MY JESUS

❦

The Third Mystery of Illumination:
Jesus Announces the Kingdom of God

INFORMAL MEDITATION

Lord, You make known to us the reward for following Your gospel teachings. Help us, O Mother, to desire the Kingdom of God.

OUR FATHER ✳ HAIL MARY 10X ✳ GLORY BE ✳

O MY JESUS

❦

The Fourth Mystery of Illumination:
The Transfiguration

INFORMAL MEDITATION

Lord, You give us once again an insight into the glory of heaven, the reward of faith. Help us to want to be with You and Your mother in the glory of heaven.

OUR FATHER * HAIL MARY 10X * GLORY BE *
O MY JESUS

The Fifth Mystery of Illumination:
The Introduction of the Holy Eucharist

INFORMAL MEDITATION

Jesus, Lord, You give us Your flesh, allowing us to be part of You, and You to be part of us. Help us, O Lord, to see You in our brothers and sisters through this greatest of all miracles, Your living flesh and blood in the Holy Eucharist.

OUR FATHER * HAIL MARY 10X * GLORY BE *
O MY JESUS

The Sorrowful Mysteries
OF THE HOLY ROSARY

(You may pray separately and begin with the standard entry prayers or with your own personal entry prayers.)

🌷

The First Sorrowful Mystery:
The Agony in the Garden

INFORMAL MEDITATION

O my dear Jesus, we know You suffered, thinking of the many souls who would not accept Your sacrifice for them. Help us to accept and to pray for those who do not.

OUR FATHER ✳ HAIL MARY 10X ✳ GLORY BE ✳

O MY JESUS

🌷

The Second Sorrowful Mystery:
Jesus is Scourged

INFORMAL MEDITATION

O my Jesus, they treat You as a common criminal and beat You unmercifully for our sins.

OUR FATHER * HAIL MARY 10X * GLORY BE *
O MY JESUS

❧

The Third Sorrowful Mystery: The Crown of Thorns

INFORMAL MEDITATION

Dearest Jesus, You are insulted, mocked, laughed at, and cruelly crowned with piercing thorns; You turn it all into a crown of glory.

OUR FATHER * HAIL MARY 10X * GLORY BE *
O MY JESUS

❧

The Fourth Sorrowful Mystery: Jesus Takes up His Cross

INFORMAL MEDITATION

Lord, help us to place our hands on Your cross, and to take up our own cross and follow You.

❧

The time it began is unclear in my mind, but somewhere after learning to pray the Rosary and then later learning of and praying the Stations of the Cross, I felt Our Lady asking that I pray each station with the Hail Mary prayers of the last two decades of the Sorrowful Mysteries. My practice was to start with this decade and then flow into the next, so that all stations would be added, and then the words of Jesus spoken from the cross. This is, again, a way to personalize and develop an intimacy with our Lord and His mother.

OUR FATHER

Jesus is condemned to death:

HAIL MARY

He takes up His cross:

HAIL MARY

He falls:

HAIL MARY

Jesus meets His mother on the path:

HAIL MARY

Simon is forced to carry the cross with Jesus:

HAIL MARY

Veronica compassionately wipes His face on
a cloth:

HAIL MARY

Jesus falls a second time:

HAIL MARY

He meets the women on the path and says,
"Weep not for Me, but for yourselves and
for your children":

HAIL MARY

Jesus falls a third time:

HAIL MARY

He is stripped of His garments:

HAIL MARY

(pause for silent contemplation)

GLORY BE ✳ O MY JESUS

❦

The Fifth Sorrowful Mystery: Jesus Is Crucified

INFORMAL MEDITATION

Jesus, please forgive us for putting You through such torture and for not realizing how our sins even today add to Your crucifixion.

❦

I remember when I had first learned how to pray the Holy Rosary, I went for a run and prayed the sorrowful mysteries. As I returned home, I began the fifth mystery of Jesus being crucified. I was so struck at the moment that I stretched out my arms in imitation of Jesus nailed to the cross and stood there, exhausted from the run, slowly praying the decade. My impromptu act didn't come close to the actual suffering of Jesus on the cross. But it was enough to sear within my heart the magnitude of the gift of redemption He gives us.

OUR FATHER

Jesus is nailed to the cross:

HAIL MARY

Jesus dies on the cross:

HAIL MARY

He is taken down from the cross:

HAIL MARY

Jesus is laid in the tomb:

HAIL MARY

"Father, forgive them":

HAIL MARY

"I thirst!":

HAIL MARY

"Woman, behold your son":

HAIL MARY

"Son, behold your mother":

HAIL MARY

"This day you will be with Me in heaven":

HAIL MARY

"It is finished; Father, into Your hands I commend My Spirit":

HAIL MARY

(pause for silent contemplation)

GLORY BE ✳ O MY JESUS

The Glorious Mysteries
OF THE HOLY ROSARY

(You may pray separately and begin with the standard entry prayers or with your own personal entry prayers.)

❧

The First Glorious Mystery:
The Resurrection

INFORMAL MEDITATION

O my God, You have risen! How we thank You for this gift of everlasting life.

OUR FATHER ✳ HAIL MARY 10X ✳ GLORY BE ✳
O MY JESUS

❧

The Second Glorious Mystery:
Jesus Ascends to the Father

INFORMAL MEDITATION

Lord, You have taken Your rightful place, until You come again in glory!

OUR FATHER ✳ HAIL MARY 10X ✳ GLORY BE ✳
O MY JESUS

The Third Glorious Mystery:
The Descent of the Holy Spirit

INFORMAL MEDITATION

Descend upon us, O Holy Spirit of God, and sanctify all that we do in thought, word, and deed.

OUR FATHER ✳ HAIL MARY 10X ✳ GLORY BE ✳
O MY JESUS

The Fourth Glorious Mystery:
The Assumption

INFORMAL MEDITATION

O Mary, conceived without sin, pray for us who have recourse to you. Help us to follow your example of holiness that we might be with you and your Son in heaven.

OUR FATHER ✳ HAIL MARY 10X ✳ GLORY BE ✳
O MY JESUS

The Fifth Glorious Mystery:
The Coronation

INFORMAL MEDITATION

Dearest Mother, you are the Queen of heaven and the Queen of our hearts!

OUR FATHER * HAIL MARY 10X * GLORY BE *
O MY JESUS

HAIL, HOLY QUEEN

(The standard ending prayer for praying the individual set of mysteries or the entire four sets of mysteries of the Holy Rosary.)

Hail holy Queen, Mother of mercy, our life, our sweetness, and our hope! To thee do we cry, poor banished children of Eve. To thee do we send up our sighs, mourning and weeping in this vale of tears.

Turn, then, most gracious advocate, thine eyes of mercy toward us, and after this our exile show unto us the blessed fruit of thy womb, Jesus. O clement, O loving, O sweet Virgin Mary.

NINE

Formal Meditations of the Holy Rosary

"Dear children: I need your prayers, now! More than ever before. I beseech you to take your rosary in your hands, now, more than ever before. Grasp it strongly, and pray with all your heart in these difficult times. Thank you for having gathered in such a number and for having responded to my call."

(Message to Mirjana on her birthday, March 18, 1992)

There are times while praying that we feel deeply immersed and can pray with fervor for what seems an eternity. These moments of what I call "freefall" prayer are timeless, with no concern about the length, or time, of prayer. The formal meditations of the Holy Rosary are like that for me.

I learned of the meditations contained here in this formal form of the Rosary prayer through a woman who had made the pilgrimage to Medjugorje and, according to her, was given the charism of locutions by Jesus and Mary. Patsy Soto has been attempting to live what she has been given, and for more than twenty years, she has spread these gifts through a special ministry she named His Teaching Ministries.

Like me, Patsy Soto was at best lukewarm in her Catholic faith, even though she strongly believed in God. The words she says she suddenly began receiving from Jesus and Mary brought her into a deep spirituality and mission, which she fought against constantly before finally accepting.

Patsy is what I refer to as a "meat and potatoes" person. No airs, no pretensions—and no background in theology. The words of the meditations speak volumes as to the authenticity of her spiritual calling.

I use selected meditations God has given her, with her permission; I feel I am called to use them. Space does not permit me to use the full text of each meditation, but they are used each time Patsy and her members gather to pray the Novena for World Peace. These special novenas convene throughout the country, and I have been privileged to be part of them on many occasions.

Here, then, are the formal meditations of the Most Holy Rosary of the Blessed Virgin Mary:

Holy Joyful Mysteries
OF THE ROSARY

OPENING

Almighty Father, I place the Precious Blood of Jesus before my lips before I pray, that my prayers may be purified before they ascend to Your divine altar.

PRAYER TO THE HOLY SPIRIT

Come, Holy Spirit, fill the hearts of Your faithful and enkindle them in the fire of Your love. Send forth Your Spirit, and they shall be created, and You shall renew the face of the earth.

PRAYER TO ST. MICHAEL

St. Michael the Archangel, defend us in battle; be our protection against the wickedness and snares of the devil. May God rebuke him, we humbly pray, and do thou, O Prince of the Heavenly Host, by the power of God, cast into Hell, Satan and all the other evil spirits who prowl throughout the world seeking the ruin of souls. Amen.

PRAYER TO OUR LADY

Blessed Virgin Mary of Guadalupe, Mother of our Lord Jesus, I call upon you this day to be my special friend here on earth, today and all the days of my life. I ask you to be my special protectress, and I place all my thoughts, words, and deeds at your feet. I ask you to be my guide and guardian, so I may please Jesus in all that I do and say.

THE CREED

I believe in God, the Father Almighty, Creator of heaven and earth, and in Jesus Christ, His only Son, our Lord, who was conceived by the Holy Spirit, born of the Virgin Mary, suffered under Pontius Pilate, was crucified, died, and was buried. He descended into hell. The third day He arose again from the dead. He ascended into heaven and is seated at the right hand of the Father. From thence He shall come to judge the living and the dead.

I believe in the Holy Spirit, the holy catholic church, the communion of saints, the forgiveness of sins, the resurrection of the body, and the life everlasting. Amen.

OUR FATHER

Our Father, who is in heaven, hallowed be Your name. Your kingdom come, Your will be done, on earth as it is in heaven.

Give us this day our daily bread, and forgive us our trespasses as we forgive those who trespass against us; and lead us not into temptation, but deliver us from evil. Amen.

HAIL MARY 3X

Hail Mary, full of grace, the Lord is with you. Blessed are you among women, and blessed is the fruit of your womb, Jesus.

Holy Mary, Mother of God, pray for us sinners, now and at the hour of our death. Amen.

GLORY BE

Glory be to the Father, the Son, and the Holy Spirit; as it was in the beginning, is now, and always will be, world without end. Amen.

❦

First Joyful Mystery: The Annunciation

Praise be to Jesus, for Jesus is Lord, Savior, Redeemer, Reconciler of all Nations!

MEDITATION FROM JESUS

Beloved little one of My Most Wounded Sacred Heart, do you see the forethought of My Father Almighty—knowing as He gave His only begotten Son to come into this world a willing Savior, through the power of the Holy Spirit, a fiat of My Blessed and Holy Virgin Mother, in order that all may have the opportunity to choose Life Eternal?

It began with the humility and mercy of My Father Almighty, the surrender of His Only Begotten Son, a surrender of My Holy Will to that of My Father Almighty, and the humility and fiat of the New Eve. My birth, a new beginning for all of humanity, is this treasure—this Gift of Life Eternal.

Yet how many of you, My children, are willing to turn away this Gift of Life Eternal, knowing full well that this grace to you was at the cost of My Life? All this I saw as I suffered alone in the garden of Gethsemane.

Your Jesus of Mercy.

OUR FATHER ✳ HAIL MARY 10X ✳ GLORY BE ✳
O MY JESUS

Jesus, Mary, and Joseph, we love you! Save souls!

Virgin Mother of Guadalupe, pray for us who have recourse to you, and obtain from your Son Jesus what we ask of you!

✤

Second Joyful Mystery:
The Visitation

Praise be to Jesus, for Jesus is Lord, Savior, Redeemer, Reconciler of All Nations!

MEDITATION FROM JESUS

My beloved children, do you not realize the power of the Holy Spirit in coming upon My beloved Elizabeth, enlightening the child in her womb to the presence of the King, the Savior of the world? The Holy Spirit empowered My Holy Mother, the Blessed Virgin, to the understanding of bringing a lowly handmaiden into the world to be not only the Temple of the Holy Spirit, but the Sanctuary of Life Eternal, and yet this was not to be without great sacrifice and condemnation. The torments My Mother would witness as the babe in her womb would be the sacrificial lamb scourged and mocked.

Your Jesus of Mercy.

OUR FATHER * HAIL MARY 10X * GLORY BE *
O MY JESUS

Jesus, Mary, and Joseph, we love you! Save souls!

Virgin Mother of Guadalupe, pray for us who have recourse to you, and obtain from your Son Jesus what we ask of you!

❧

Third Joyful Mystery:
The Birth of Our Lord Jesus Christ

Praise be to Jesus, for Jesus is Lord, Savior, Redeemer, Reconciler of All Nations!

MEDITATION FROM JESUS

As you make this journey with Me on this third mystery, realize the insignificance of a manger. Yet this manger was to be the birth-place of a king—the birthplace of the Son of God. Yes, it was the place where stray animals slept and where the walls of the manger were the heavenly skies that surrounded the manger. The light was the stars gleaming from the sky. I, the King, had no place to lay My head, except for the mixture of the earth and grass that grew wildly in the land.

But I, who am the Son of God, the Almighty, who created all, was to show all mankind it would not be the palaces of the earth that would house the King, the Son of God, nor the gems of the world that would trim the robe I was to wear—for I was not to be considered a King in this world, and My throne was not to be made of gold—but instead would be made of wood. And in the end, it would not be a crown of jewels they would place on Me—but a crown of thorns piercing My head. I would not be clothed in fine silk— but draped in a purple cloth found in the dirt. I would not be addressed as "Son of God." Instead, I would be mocked and spat upon— the crowds calling not for my reign on this earth—but calling out that I, Jesus, "King of the Jews," should be crucified.

This was allowed for each of you, My beloved children, out of My love and the love of God, the Father Almighty. I became the Sacrificial Lamb for each of you. This is how much you are loved.

Your Jesus of Mercy.

OUR FATHER * HAIL MARY 10X * GLORY BE *
O MY JESUS

Jesus, Mary, and Joseph, we love you! Save souls!

Virgin Mother of Guadalupe, pray for us who have recourse to you, and obtain from your Son Jesus what we ask of you!

Fourth Joyful Mystery:
The Presentation

Praise be to Jesus, for Jesus is Lord, Savior, Redeemer, Reconciler of All Nations!

MEDITATION FROM JESUS

Beloved children of My Most Wounded Sacred Heart, as it was written in the Law of the Lord—presenting Me to the Lord—this, done with love: Do you realize as I hung on the cross of salvation, humanity would present Me to My Lord with the inscription hanging over my head in mockery, "This is the King of the Jews!"? How many times have you, My children, mocked through sin the Father Almighty?

Your Jesus of Mercy.

OUR FATHER ✳ HAIL MARY 10X ✳ GLORY BE ✳
O MY JESUS

Jesus, Mary, and Joseph, we love you! Save souls!

Virgin Mother of Guadalupe, pray for us who have recourse to you, and obtain from your Son Jesus what we ask of you!

✷

Fifth Joyful Mystery:
The Finding of the Child Jesus in the Temple

Praise be to Jesus, for Jesus is Lord, Savior, Redeemer, Reconciler of All Nations!

MEDITATION FROM JESUS

Beloved children of My Most Wounded Sacred Heart, here I stand in the middle of all the teachers, understanding and teaching at My young age, because of the wisdom of My Father, only to be crucified through the High Priest and learned men asking for the death of the Sacrificial Lamb. They had waited all these years for the Messiah, and yet they refused to see that I—the Messiah—was in their midst. Will you be aware when I AM in your midst . . . or will you remain blinded by evil?
Your Jesus of Mercy.

OUR FATHER * HAIL MARY 10X * GLORY BE *
O MY JESUS

Jesus, Mary, and Joseph, we love you! Save souls!

Virgin Mother of Guadalupe, pray for us who have recourse to you, and obtain from your Son Jesus what we ask of you!

Holy Luminous Mysteries
OF THE ROSARY

(If praying only these mysteries, use the same opening prayers as found in the beginning of the Holy Joyful Mysteries.)

First Luminous Mystery:
Jesus' Baptism in the Jordan

Praise be to Jesus, for Jesus is Lord, Savior, Redeemer, and Reconciler of All Nations!

MEDITATION FROM JESUS

Beloved children of My Most Wounded Sacred Heart, as the Holy Spirit came upon My Holy Mother overshadowing her, in order that I, the Son of the Almighty, come into this world, and when I knelt in prayer as the Holy Spirit came upon Me, it was at this time My Father spoke to Me that He was pleased with Me. Do you not realize, at the time of your baptism, it is also in a very special way that the Holy Spirit comes upon each of you? This grace, so many have turned away from by not being baptized or not having their children baptized.

How can your souls be a temple for the Holy Spirit to reside in when so many souls are darkened with the stain of sin, and when so many souls still remain in original sin because they have not received the sacrament of Baptism? How many of your children's children have not been baptized because they feel this is so unnecessary, or have not been taught how truly necessary the sacrament of Baptism truly is?

Oh, My children, you are being called. Are you listening? Do not close your hearts and ears to My pleas, for you do not know the hour you will be called home. Are you prepared, My children? Are your children prepared to come before Me? Remember, My Children, I AM your Jesus of Mercy.

OUR FATHER ✳ HAIL MARY 10X ✳ GLORY BE ✳
O MY JESUS

Jesus, Mary, and Joseph, we love you! Save souls!

Virgin Mother of Guadalupe, pray for us who have recourse to you, and obtain from your Son Jesus what we ask of you!

✵

Second Luminous Mystery: Jesus' Self-Manifestation at the Wedding of Cana

Praise be to Jesus, for Jesus is Lord, Savior, Redeemer, and Reconciler of All Nations!

MEDITATION FROM JESUS

Look back through history, and if history has taught you anything, then remember this point in history: consider the Son of God, a King coming into this world—a simple man, born in a manger to a virgin, and as this boy grows into a man—He and His mother are at a wedding feast, but the people have run out of wine. Now, this mother knows that her son, the Son of God the Father, Creator of all, can do something about this. He can turn water into wine because He is the Son of God. But He isn't asked to do this to prove that He is the Son of God. No, My children, it is a simple matter of trusting as well as an act of obedience, love, and kindness.

Your Jesus of Mercy.

OUR FATHER * HAIL MARY 10X * GLORY BE *
O MY JESUS

Jesus, Mary, and Joseph, we love you! Save souls!

Virgin Mother of Guadalupe, pray for us who have recourse to you, and obtain from your Son Jesus what we ask of you!

❦

Third Luminous Mystery:
Jesus' Proclamation of the Kingdom of
God with His Call to Conversion

Praise be to Jesus, for Jesus is Lord, Savior, Redeemer, and Reconciler of All Nations!

MEDITATION FROM JESUS

Peace, My beloved ones, to each of you and your children! Thank you, My beloved little one, for opening your heart to me on this day. I know the sadness you feel at not having your father on this earth with you, but as I have told you, he is where the love is eternal and My presence is his eternal light.

I thank you for remaining obedient to my call and My invitation at giving these words to My Holy Mother's Rosary of the Luminous Mysteries on this day in honor of My Father, Abba Father King. My Father has given you free will, freedom of choice, and you have squandered the many soul-saving gifts, and yet He continues to give you each His Love Eternal. What will it take to make you see the many daily ravages of your lifestyle of sin dissipate your souls and the souls of your children? I love you, My children. Pray, My children. Pray! I love you. Your Jesus of Mercy.

OUR FATHER ✳ HAIL MARY 10X ✳ GLORY BE ✳
O MY JESUS

Jesus, Mary, and Joseph, we love you! Save souls!

Virgin Mother of Guadalupe, pray for us who have recourse to you, and obtain from your Son Jesus what we ask of you!

❦

Fourth Luminous Mystery: Jesus' Transfiguration

Praise be to Jesus, for Jesus is Lord, Savior, Redeemer, and Reconciler of All Nations!

MEDITATION FROM JESUS

Beloved little one of My Most Wounded Sacred Heart, in this meditation I speak to you of the "Teachings"—the graces abundantly showered upon Me from My Father, upon My disciples, and most important upon each of you, My children. Here I give you words, "Teachings," as when My Father gave Me the grace of My Transfiguration, when He brought Me before the teachers in the temple to give them "Teachings," when I stood with My disciples and with Moses and Elias, words spoken, "Teachings," given then and now. The difference is that My disciples listened!

I, Jesus your Christ, listened to Moses and Elias, to My Father as He acknowledged Me as His Son and invited all to listen to Me. Yet you, My children, remain with deaf ears to My Words, to My Scripture, and you see that, because you have not listened, the world you live in may be your own demise.

Oh, My children, what good are my words if they go to deaf ears? But I do not stop, neither does My Father Almighty, nor My Holy Mother who pleads for each of you to My Father. I love you, my children.
Your Jesus of Mercy.

OUR FATHER ✳ HAIL MARY 10X ✳ GLORY BE ✳
O MY JESUS

Jesus, Mary, and Joseph, we love you! Save souls!

Virgin Mother of Guadalupe, pray for us who have recourse to you, and obtain from your Son Jesus what we ask of you!

✣

Fifth Luminous Mystery:
Jesus' Institution of the Eucharist
as the Sacramental Expression
of the Paschal Mystery

Praise be to Jesus, for Jesus is Lord, Savior, Redeemer, and Reconciler of All Nations!

MEDITATION FROM JESUS

I stood before My apostles on the eve of My crucifixion knowing that I was to give My life for each of you, not only on the Cross, but I gave Myself and continue to give Myself entirely to each of you in My True Presence in the form of bread and wine—My Body, My Blood. This is how much I love each of you. In how many ways can I say and prove this to you?

And, as I stood in the midst of the teachers doing My Father's work, I stand in your midst again doing My Father's work as He so readily desires to give you Life Eternal—I so desire to give you Myself, the Bread of Life. And so we come again to your decision on My invitation, and I ask that you not make this decision lightly—for My Father gave Me, His Only Begotten Son, given totally for you, in order that all may have Life Eternal. Just as with every time you come to receive Me in the sacrament of the Holy Eucharist, I again give you My whole being. Do you desire to remain in darkness instead of in My Light? Why do you continue to disregard Mine and My Father's gifts to you? I love you, My children. I AM your Jesus of Mercy.

OUR FATHER ✳ HAIL MARY 10X ✳ GLORY BE ✳
O MY JESUS

Jesus, Mary, and Joseph, we love you! Save souls!

Virgin Mother of Guadalupe, pray for us who have recourse to you, and obtain from your Son Jesus what we ask of you!

❧

Holy Sorrowful Mysteries
OF THE ROSARY

(If praying only these mysteries, use the same opening prayers as found in the beginning of the Holy Joyful Mysteries.)

❧

First Sorrowful Mystery:
The Agony in the Garden

Praise be to Jesus, for Jesus is Lord, Savior, Redeemer, and Reconciler of All nations!

MEDITATION FROM JESUS

Beloved children of My Most Wounded Sacred Heart, I have given you these meditations for each mystery of this, My Scriptural Rosary, in order that you may reflect on My life, death, resurrection, and My light of mercy through My works on this earth. For luminous means light, and I AM the truth, the life, the light, and the WAY to Eternal Life for all.

It is only in surrendering your will to Me that you will truly have peace. It is My desire, My invitation to you—this journey with Me, through Me, for Me—that you may understand this Holy Way of My Cross and be brought to a true encounter and relationship with Me, for I will not only guide you, but lead you and yours to Eternal Life. But you have a free will, as also My apostles had in their invitation to stay with Me and pray on the eve of My crucifixion.

You would think, knowing what My apostles did with My invitation, that it would dissuade a repeated reenactment of their behavior; and their sadness and regret of this night would change the hearts of all. But the evil that was to overcome the world in those days and the days ahead, the hate and anger of those who would persecute Me then, continues in these times.

Realize, My children, the unbearable pain My Holy Mother would encounter as she would see Me with thorns on My head as My crown, blood-soaked, and a torn purple cape draping My Body, dressing the King and Son of God, the Almighty, and My staff being the cross, which I would drag alone on the Via Dolorosa, till I would fall from the pain and exhaustion, and Simon would then be told to help Me.

Your Jesus Crucified.

OUR FATHER ✳ HAIL MARY 10X ✳ GLORY BE ✳
O MY JESUS

Jesus, Mary, and Joseph, we love you! Save souls!

Virgin Mother of Guadalupe, pray for us who have recourse to you, and obtain from your Son Jesus what we ask of you!

✤

Second Sorrowful Mystery:
The Scourging at the Pillar

Praise be to Jesus, for Jesus is Lord, Savior, Redeemer, and Reconciler of All Nations.

MEDITATION OF JESUS

Oh My beloved little one, it is difficult when you are hurt because someone close to you hurts you through words or actions. It is even more difficult to understand because you want to be an example of love to others, but during these trying times it becomes harder to be kind and you wonder why your anger gets the best of you. Oh My children, remember you are human, and it will and can only be through a stronger prayer life, in Me, with Me, and through Me, that you will be able to walk this difficult journey of the Via Dolorosa.

The bitterness and pain of this life may be like the hateful and evil behavior of the soldiers who beat and scourged Me and the townsfolk who mocked and spat at Me. As I forgave all for what was done to Me, I ask that you forgive each other, and as I love all, My desire for you is to love all people. This is what I ask from each of you.

Even as difficult as life becomes, this is what you must always strive for, and if you call out to Me, I will always be there for you, I will never turn away from you, I will always love you, even when you aren't able to do what I have asked of you, because this is how much I love each one of you.

Your Jesus of Mercy.

OUR FATHER ✳ HAIL MARY 10X ✳ GLORY BE ✳
O MY JESUS

Jesus, Mary, and Joseph, we love you! Save souls!

Virgin Mother of Guadalupe, pray for us who have recourse to you, and obtain from your Son Jesus what we ask of you!

❧

Third Sorrowful Mystery:
The Crowning of Thorns

Praise be to Jesus, for Jesus is Lord, Savior, Redeemer, Reconciler of All Nations!

MEDITATION FROM JESUS

Beloved little one of My Most Wounded Sacred Heart, think of the excruciating pain as the thorns were pushed harder and harder to penetrate My head by the soldier who mocked and laughed that he was crowning a king. This soldier, one of many whom I forgave and even when he continually put pressure on the crown of thorns piercing my sacred head, I begged forgiveness of My Father for this soldier.

Do you, My children, beg forgiveness of My Father for the sins of mankind in this world, even when their sins affect you and your children? It is only forgiveness, love, prayer, and sacrifice for each other that can overshadow the presence of sin and evil in this world.

Imagine the sorrow and pain My Holy Mother went through as she saw her Son, a King, the Son that the Angel Gabriel had said would be great and would be called the Son of the Most High. Yet, here He was being crowned with thorns instead of a crown of jewels. My Holy Mother stood by watching and praying—her prayers being lifted to the Father Almighty, asking forgiveness for what they were doing to her Son, to the Son of the Father Almighty. Remember her example, My children. Remember her love, My children. Remember her fiat, My children. Pray, My children. Pray!

Your Jesus of Mercy.

OUR FATHER ✳ HAIL MARY 10X ✳ GLORY BE ✳
O MY JESUS

Jesus, Mary, and Joseph, we love you! Save souls!

Virgin Mother of Guadalupe, pray for us who have recourse to you, and obtain from your Son Jesus what we ask of you!

Fourth Sorrowful Mystery:
The Carrying of the Cross

Praise be to Jesus, for Jesus is Lord, Savior, Redeemer, and Reconciler of All Nations!

MEDITATION FROM JESUS

Listen, My children, and continue to reflect on My Holy Mother as she stood there remembering the words from the Angel Gabriel asking her not to be afraid. Yet, on this sorrowful day, before her I walked, her Son, scourged, beaten, a crown of thorns piercing My head, and barely able to drag the cross I was to be crucified on. Here I was, passing her by, looking into her eyes with such love. I, her loving Son, whom she cared for, watched over—her baby.

And when the days of her purification were fulfilled according to the law of Moses, they took Me to Jerusalem to present Me to the Lord, as it is written in the Law of the Lord. Here we were together again, and she would again present Me to the Lord, but this time on a road called the Via Dolorosa—not a day of joy, but a day of sorrow, as I walked to My death to be crucified.

As I passed her by, looking into her eyes, I will never forget the love, comfort, strength and sorrow I saw in her eyes, in those eyes that cry tears again for her children—especially those being lost to the error of sin, souls forever lost. But with your prayers and sacrifice, they can still be touched. Will you, My children,

soothe her tears, soothe My wounds, pray, sacrifice, and surrender to our call?
Your Jesus of Mercy.

OUR FATHER * HAIL MARY 10X * GLORY BE *
O MY JESUS

Jesus, Mary, and Joseph, we love you! Save souls!

Virgin Mother of Guadalupe, pray for us who have recourse to you, and obtain from your Son Jesus what we ask of you!

❦

Fifth Sorrowful Mystery:
The Crucifixion

Praise be to Jesus, for Jesus is Lord, Savior, Redeemer and Reconciler of All Nations!

MEDITATION FROM JESUS

Oh, My children, are you prepared? Are you ready to stand before Me, before My Father? For all must come to this day. Remember how, for the last time, My Holy Mother looked back, remembering how she questioned the Angel Gabriel, how was this all to happen? This plan of the Father now was coming to pass. All in His Time and in His Will.

And, yes, the pain was tremendous, but knowing that she had given her fiat, as her Son had given His fiat, we had accepted the Father's perfect Will. As when a wheat grain falls into the earth and dies, it remains only a single grain. But if it dies, it yields a rich harvest. I, your Jesus of Mercy, Son of the Father, gave My fiat in order that all may have Life Eternal.

My Holy Mother stood before My cross as I hung there for the salvation of all mankind. I gave her to you, My children, from the cross, as I said to her, "Woman, behold thy son," and to My beloved disciple, John, I said, "Behold thy mother."

It was not enough that I gave you My Mother. No, My children, I gave My life for each of you! I love you, My children. I Am your Jesus of Mercy. I am your Jesus Crucified.

OUR FATHER * HAIL MARY 10X * GLORY BE *
O MY JESUS

Jesus, Mary, and Joseph, we love you! Save souls!

Virgin Mother of Guadalupe, pray for us who have recourse to you, and obtain from your Son Jesus what we ask of you!

Holy Glorious Mysteries
OF THE ROSARY

(If praying only these mysteries, use the same opening prayers as found in the beginning of the Holy Joyful Mysteries.)

First Glorious Mystery:
The Resurrection

Praise be to Jesus, for Jesus is Lord, Savior, Redeemer, and Reconciler of All Nations!

MEDITATION FROM JESUS

Welcome, beloved little one of My Most Wounded Sacred Heart. Thank you for opening your heart to My words, that you may hear with the ears of the soul and see with the eyes of the soul. It was now time for the Holy Spirit to pour forth His Spirit unto My apostles, but first they must see for themselves that that which was prophesied was to come to pass. Simon Peter came to see for himself that I, the Lord Jesus Christ, Rabboni, his teacher, who was crucified and died, now had risen to fulfill the prophecy and save the people from their sins, as foretold by an angel to My beloved earthly father, Joseph.

Joseph, who could have easily refused to take My Holy Mother as his wife, instead opened his heart to the Will of God, My Father Almighty. It was through a willingness, a surrender of My earthly father Joseph's will, attesting to the strength of faith and love he had for God, My Father Almighty, that Joseph accepted what was given to him in his dream.

Whereas even though Simon Peter heard My words in which I had spoken to him of betraying Me three times, through his pride, he would not listen. It was pride and fear that overcame his will.

Think about this, My beloved children, when the sin of pride gets in the way of your spiritual growth or causes you to abstain from the sacrament of Reconciliation, where you receive the grace of absolution in order that your soul once again becomes the temple of the Holy Spirit.

Your Jesus of Mercy.

OUR FATHER * HAIL MARY 10X * GLORY BE *
O MY JESUS

Jesus, Mary, and Joseph, we love you! Save souls!

Virgin Mother of Guadalupe, pray for us who have recourse to you, and obtain from your Son Jesus what we ask of you!

❦

Second Glorious Mystery: The Ascension of Jesus into Heaven

Praise be to Jesus, for Jesus is Lord, Savior, Redeemer, and Reconciler of all Nations!

MEDITATION FROM JESUS

Beloved little one of My Most Wounded Sacred Heart, thank you once again for opening your heart to My words, listening with the ears of your soul, and seeing with the eyes of your soul.

You ask Me how there is a correlation in the mystery of My Ascension and the visitation of My Holy Mother to My beloved Elizabeth. Realize, daughter, that in opening the heart to the promptings of the Holy Spirit, as I said earlier, graces boundlessly will flow, surrendering the will to the Holy Will of My Father Almighty.

Zachary was told by the angel that Elizabeth would bear him a son who was to be called

John, who would be filled with the Holy Spirit even from his mother's womb. It was this plan for the salvation of mankind that brought forth the Holy Spirit upon Zachary, Elizabeth, John the Baptist—predecessors through prayer, sacrifice, and a surrendering of the will to the Holy Will of My Father Almighty.

Abba Father's plan for the salvation of the souls of humanity is to have Eternal Life. As John had said, "that it was he who baptized with water," and as he saw the Holy Spirit descending upon Me—"who would baptize with the Holy Spirit."

Your Jesus of Mercy.

OUR FATHER ✳ HAIL MARY 10X ✳ GLORY BE ✳
O MY JESUS

Jesus, Mary, and Joseph, we love you! Save souls!

Virgin Mother of Guadalupe, pray for us who have recourse to you, and obtain from your Son Jesus what we ask of you!

❦

Third Glorious Mystery: The Descent of the Holy Spirit upon the Apostles

Praise be to Jesus, for Jesus is Lord, Savior, Redeemer, and Reconciler of All Nations!

MEDITATION FROM JESUS

Thank you, My beloved little one, for opening your heart to My words. I, Who was conceived by the Holy Spirit, born of the Virgin Mary, spoke to My apostles of the day as promised by My Father. They were to be clothed with the power from on high, the Holy Spirit, as My Holy Mother was spoken to by the Angel Gabriel that "the Holy Spirit shall come upon thee and the power of the Most High shall overshadow thee."

And so it was that My Father's Holy Will came to pass, that all mankind be given the Mercy of the Father Almighty—not taking your free will, but giving you the choice, My children, not to perish in the flames of eternal perdition but to choose Eternal Life. These words were spoken through the prophets of Truth. For I, Who AM, came to give you Life Eternal. I AM Truth!

I was born in a manger—risen from the dead in order to give you the choice for Life

Eternal—and stood in the midst of My apostles and spoke to Thomas, "Bring here thy finger, and see my hands; and bring here thy hand, and put it into My side; and be not unbelieving; but believing."

Now, I say to you, My children, as you read these words, I am asking you to change your ways, to return to Me, for I Am Truth, Love, Mercy, and I desire that you be with Me for *all eternity*. Are you, as did My doubting Thomas, doubting these, My words? Ponder seriously why I come to give you these words. Then ask yourselves, what are the choices you are making? What are the examples you are setting? I love you, My children.

Your Jesus of Mercy.

OUR FATHER ✳ HAIL MARY 10X ✳ GLORY BE ✳
O MY JESUS

Jesus, Mary, and Joseph, we love you! Save souls!

Virgin Mother of Guadalupe, pray for us who have recourse to you, and obtain from your Son Jesus what we ask of you!

❦

Fourth Glorious Mystery:
The Assumption of Mary into Heaven

Praise be to Jesus, for Jesus is Lord, Savior, Redeemer, and Reconciler of All Nations!

MEDITATIONS FROM JESUS

Beloved children of My Most Wounded Sacred Heart, how I must emphasize the need for mankind to return to My Holy Sacraments, to prayer, to sacrifice, to surrendering your wills to the Holy Will of the Father Almighty. For it is only through prayer, sacrifice, and surrendering your wills that graces may open the hearts of the many souls that are being lost through sin, which abounds in this world. And take the example of My Holy Mother who was assumed— body, blood, soul—because of her selfless love, not only for Me, Her Son, but for all her children; the release of her will, her surrender of her will to the perfect Holy Will of My Father Almighty.

Even as she was being told by Simeon that a sword was to pierce her heart, these words did not change her decision to accept the Holy Will of My Father Almighty. On the contrary, she embraced with love the

Almighty Will of My Father, knowing in her heart that all that Simeon prophesied had been revealed to him by the Holy Spirit and was to come to pass. Imagine how Simeon felt realizing after so many years in waiting for the Messiah that this woman who stood before him was carrying the infant who is the salvation of all humanity. Contemplate now what would have been if My Holy Mother had not surrendered her will to the Holy Will of the Father Almighty. Contemplate now what your surrender, your prayers, and your sacrifice will mean not only to your souls, but to the souls of your children, your families, your world.

Your Jesus of Mercy.

OUR FATHER ✳ HAIL MARY 10X ✳ GLORY BE ✳
O MY JESUS

Jesus, Mary, and Joseph, we love you! Save souls!

Virgin Mother of Guadalupe, pray for us who have recourse to you, and obtain from your Son Jesus what we ask of you!

❦

Fifth Glorious Mystery:
The Coronation of Mama Mary

Praise be to Jesus, for Jesus is Lord, Savior, Redeemer, and Reconciler of All Nations!

MEDITATION FROM JESUS

Beloved little one of My Most Wounded Sacred Heart, thank you for opening your heart to My words. To enter into My Kingdom for all eternity is what all My children should desire, and you would think that with what they are seeing in this world of chaos, confusion, hate, anger, that My children would do all in their power to attain Eternal Life, with Me, through Me, for Me.

BUT that is not the case, My little one. The anxiousness, hurriedness, uneasiness—this all comes from the worldly ways, and yet My children do not realize this, nor do they even understand what My peace, My love, My gentleness, My patience, My mercy can be in their lives. So they continue on in their worldly, materialistic lives, blinded to My Truths.

My Holy Mother was crowned Queen of Heaven and Earth because she, as no other human, could and would always relinquish *totally* to the Holy Will of My Father Almighty.

She surrendered not only her will, but her life to the Holy Will of My Father Almighty.

Imagine her pain in realizing I, her Son, was not in the caravan with her, nor with My father. The fear she must have felt at knowing that I, her Son, was lost, and not only lost, but to be aware that I was lost among those that could turn against Me and betray Me—to those who wanted My death, yet still knowing that she must accept the Holy Will of God, the Father Almighty. The pain and realization that even though she was the mother of the Son of God, the Messiah, her Son's life would not be one of royalty, but of suffering, and in the end, even death in order that all humanity would be given the choice for Life Eternal.

How many of you, My children, would remain silent and obedient to a request of giving the life of your child so that others would have the opportunity to CHOOSE to save or NOT save their souls?

Your Jesus of Mercy.

OUR FATHER ✳ HAIL MARY 10X ✳ GLORY BE ✳
O MY JESUS

Jesus, Mary, and Joseph, we love you! Save souls!

Virgin Mother of Guadalupe, pray for us who have recourse to you, and obtain from your Son Jesus what we ask of you!

HAIL, HOLY QUEEN

THE MEMORARE

Remember, O Most Gracious Virgin Mary, that never was it known, that anyone who fled to your protection, implored your help, or sought your intercession, was left unaided. Inspired by this confidence, we fly unto you, O Virgin of virgins, our mother. To you do we come; before you we stand, sinful and sorrowful. O Mother of the Word Incarnate, despise not our petitions, but in your mercy, hear and answer us. Amen.

TEN

My Special Morning Prayers

"It is up to you to pray and to persevere. I have made promises to you; also be without anxiety. Faith will not know how to be alive without prayer. Pray more."

(Message given October 10, 1981)

Without question, the prayers that I give you in this chapter are probably the most important in this book. They are prayers that, I believe, Mary purposefully placed in my heart. She states in the above message, *"I have made promises to you!"* Well, I too made promises to her, and one was to spread these extremely important prayers. She has called me to share these special prayers with you so that their special healing grace can be utilized.

Why has it taken me so long to respond to Our Lady's request to make known these prayers she gave to me? I do not know. I began receiving them very early in my mission. Perhaps I personally needed to develop them and utilize them in order to gain full insight as to their power.

Early in my travels to Medjugorje I learned the power of a basic prayer that Mary had given to the visionaries, consisting of a traditional, regional way of saying seven sets of Our Father, Hail Mary, and Glory Be. She then told them to add the Creed, stating, *"It is my favorite prayer!"*

The fourth day of her apparitions in Medjugorje, Mary gave the visionaries this sequence of prayers to be used for many different petitions of prayer, telling them: *"Continue to recite the Lord's Prayer, the Hail Mary, and the Glory Be seven times, but also add the Creed"* (June 27, 1981).

This would continue to be a recommendation by the Lady of Medjugorje; she gave this message on April 24, 1982, when asked by the people through the visionaries what needs to be done in order to have more cures: *"Pray! Pray and believe firmly. Say the prayers which have already been requested* (the Lord's Prayer, the Hail Mary, and the Glory Be seven times each, and the Creed). *Do more penance."* Again, two months later on July 21, concerning cures: *"For the cure of the sick, it is important to say the following prayers: the Creed, and seven times each, the Lord's Prayer, the Hail Mary, and the Glory Be, and to fast on bread and water."* In the same message, she added, *"It is good to impose one's hands on the sick and to pray. It is good to anoint the sick with Holy oil."*

As if these examples were not enough to show that this prayer of the seven Our Fathers, Hail Marys, and Glory Bes, is a cure-all, Mary added this message concerning the holy souls of purgatory, also on April 21, 1982: *"There are many souls in Purgatory. There are also persons who have been consecrated to God—some priests, some religious. Pray for their intentions, at least the Lord's Prayer, the Hail Mary, and the Glory Be seven times each, and the Creed. I recommend it to you. There is a large number of souls who have been in purgatory for a long time because no one prays for them."*

These last messages support what I wrote earlier in this book about how we may answer our own prayers by using the holy power given to us. Mary told the visionaries and the villagers to use this special prayer for spiritual and physical healings, for the priests, for the souls of purgatory, for general and individual peace, and for many other things.

Then Our Lady personalized the prayers for me by giving me special intentions to be prayed in between the Our Father, Hail Mary, and Glory Be sets. It happened over a period of time and *I was totally unaware* that she was doing it! Then later, looking back on the receipt and use of the petitions, I realized that she was giving me an even more powerful in-depth cure for the ills of the world, as well as for specific needs of individuals.

Without further discussion, let me recount the wonderful prayer that I now pray every morning.

My Special Morning Prayers

OPENING PRAYER

All praise, honor, and glory to You, Lord
Jesus Christ, King of eternal glory. Send down
Your Holy Spirit through the intercession of
the Blessed Virgin Mary, Your well-beloved
spouse.

THE CREED

O MY JESUS

O my Jesus, forgive us our sins; save us from
the fires of hell. Lead all souls to heaven, and
help especially those who are in need of Your
mercy. Amen.

THE DIVINE MERCY OPENING

Eternal Father, I offer You the body and
blood, soul and divinity, of Your dearly
beloved Son, our Lord and Savior, Jesus
Christ, in atonement for our sins and those of
the whole world. For the sake of His sorrowful passion, have mercy on us and on the
whole world.

MEDITATION FOR THE FIRST
SEQUENCE OF PRAYERS

Through the Immaculate Heart of Mary to
the Sacred Heart of Jesus, I pray for the

pagan, the heathen, the atheist, and the agnostic, the weak and the fallen away; and for all of us who have failed You time and again. I pray for the children of the world, for their guidance, protection, and conversion; and I pray against the sins that take us away from Your grace, especially the sins of the flesh: abortion, promiscuity, pornography, lust, temptation, addiction, avarice, and greed—and above all, pride.

OUR FATHER * HAIL MARY * GLORY BE

MEDITATION FOR THE SECOND
SEQUENCE OF PRAYERS

Through the Immaculate Heart of Mary to the Sacred Heart of Jesus, I pray for the souls of purgatory, each and every one, to enter into the kingdom of heaven. I pray for my family of all generations, for those whom I have known in this lifetime and, most especially, for those souls who have no one to pray for them. Moreover, I ask the holy souls of purgatory to pray for those of us left in this exile.

OUR FATHER * HAIL MARY * GLORY BE

MEDITATION FOR THE THIRD

SEQUENCE OF PRAYERS

Through the Immaculate Heart of Mary to the Sacred Heart of Jesus, I pray for our church, for its holiness, its guidance and protection, its preservation; and for the unity of all faiths into one. I pray for Pope Benedict XVI, for his health, his intentions, and the fulfillment of his mission; for the loyalty of the entire church, and for good, strong vocations, true to the teachings of the church; and for those priests and religious whom I have known, especially _____ (here I list those special priests I am asked to pray for specifically by name; you may list your own favorites whom you feel you should pray for). I pray for Father Gobbi and the entire Marian Movement of Priests, for all of the Franciscans of Medjugorje and all priests who have made pilgrimage to Medjugorje, and, most especially, for the Bishop of Mostar to open his heart to the truth of the apparitions.

OUR FATHER * HAIL MARY * GLORY BE

MEDITATION FOR THE FOURTH
SEQUENCE OF PRAYERS

I pray for all those souls whom I have taken into my heart from all the places where Our Lady has sent me, and their families and those whom they pray for; and I ask the Holy Spirit to heal those suffering from diseases and conditions, all for the great glory of God, the will of God, and then for our needs. I especially pray for _____ (list all those whom you pray for; my list is added to and decreased, based on the results over a period of time).

OUR FATHER * HAIL MARY * GLORY BE

MEDITATION FOR THE FIFTH
SEQUENCE OF PRAYERS

I pray for all families everywhere, especially those poor families who have suffered and died for their faith, through the sins of abortion, war, terrorism, apathy, high crimes, addictions, slavery, and all of the evil turned loose in the world by Satan and his demons. I pray for my family, my spouse, my children, my parents, and all members of our extended family. (I list here the individual names of my immediate family and other family members in need.)

OUR FATHER * HAIL MARY * GLORY BE

Before the next two sequences of prayer, the beginning of my meditation changes, and I add, "I pray to the Father, the Son, and the Holy Spirit." I can only guess as to why these two sequences begin differently, but it is what I feel Our Lady has asked me to do, possibly because of the power of grace generated from and to each of them.

MEDITATION FOR THE SIXTH
SEQUENCE OF PRAYERS

I pray to the Father, the Son, and the Holy Spirit, in thanksgiving for the great grace of the apparitions in Medjugorje, for allowing the Blessed Virgin Mary to come daily for so long. May they continue until their fulfillment. I pray for the visionaries and their families: Marija, Vicka, Mirjana, Ivanka, Ivan, and Jakov; and for locutionaries Jelena and Marijana; also, for _____. (Here I list other visionaries and locutionists whom I feel Our Lady has asked me to pray for daily. You may do the same for any individual with such a charism you feel God has asked you to pray for.) I pray for all of the priests and religious in Medjugorje who lead the people, for all of the villagers, and for all those who have come and found conversion. I pray for a renewal of the mission the Lord has given me, to spread the messages of Medjugorje.

OUR FATHER * HAIL MARY * GLORY BE

Of all the meditations given me for this special morning prayer, this seventh is the most revealing, mainly because of the many saints Our Lady has placed in my heart to assist in my mission. I knew only one saint early in the mission, and that was St. Therese of the Child Jesus, more popularly known as the "Little Flower." As the prayer developed, Our Lady continued adding saints over time; first, St. Joseph, and then my patron saint, St. John the Evangelist. Next were some of the disciples, and it continued until I had an entire litany of saints! I stress again, I was unaware of her adding these names to the prayer. One day I realized that my seven Our Father, Hail Mary, and Glory Be prayers of Medjugorje were no longer just a six-minute prayer!

Contributing to my amazement at this special prayer is that saints and holy people are still added from time to time. The latest—

possibly no real surprise—is Pope John Paul II, whom Our Lady has given me as John Paul the Great.

Here, then, is the most potent of the seven sequences:

MEDITATION FOR THE SEVENTH
SEQUENCE OF PRAYERS

To the Father, Son, and Holy Spirit, great praise and thanksgiving for the grace You have given us of Jesus in the Holy Eucharist.

We thank You for His divine mercy.

We thank You for our church and all of its sacraments.

And, we thank You for allowing the most Blessed Virgin Mary to come to earth in apparition to confirm the Gospels for us; for all past and present apparitions, most especially in Medjugorje.

Thank you, St. Joseph, Holy Spouse of the Blessed Virgin Mary, putative father of Jesus, and powerful saint in your own right.

Thank you, Little Flower, St. Therese; help me to be a saint and to be pure and holy.

Thank you, St. Elizabeth Anne Seton; please help me in the conversion of souls.

And thank you, St. Francis,

St. Clare,
St. Bernadette,
St. Brigitte,
St. Mary Magdalene,
St. Maximilian Kolbe,
St. Louis De Monfort,
St. Augustine,
St. Monica,
St. Maria Goretti,
St. Frances Cabrini,
St. Peter,
St. Paul,
St. John,
St. Jude,
St. Anthony,
St. Anne,
St. Padre Pio,
St. Faustina,
St. Philomena,
St. Francis de Sales,
Blessed Mother Teresa,
Holy Maria Valtorta,
and Holy John Paul the Great.

The litany of saints began with the top three,
and for some reason they were to be separate
from the rest. At first, it was simply Our Lady,

St. Joseph, and St. Therese who composed my litany of saints. Other saints were added quietly, and later, St. Elizabeth Anne Seton was removed from the general list and moved into the top group. I think it is because she was a convert like me!

The point is this: once we open our hearts to heaven and become children of God, He will give us all the help we need to continue our conversion and to be a Jesus to our brothers and sisters. We truly become a part of the entire "Communion of Saints."

The seventh sequence of prayers continues:

St. Michael, St. Gabriel, and St. Raphael, powerful archangels, be with us, and guide us in these times of great trial:

St. Michael the Archangel, defend us in battle; be our safeguard against the wickedness and snares of the devil. May God rebuke him, we humbly pray; and do you, O prince of the heavenly host, by the power of God, cast into hell Satan and all of his evil spirits, who prowl through the world seeking the ruin of souls. Amen.

Holy guardian angel, be with us at all times, and keep us on the path of holiness.

OUR FATHER * HAIL MARY * GLORY BE

ADDED PRAYER AT THE END
OF THE SEVEN SEQUENCES

O my Jesus, forgive us our sins, save us from the fires of hell, lead all souls to heaven, and help especially those who are most in need of Your mercy.

CLOSING PRAYERS

Hail holy Queen, Mother of mercy, our life, our sweetness, and our hope! To thee do we cry, poor banished children of Eve. To thee do we send up our sighs, mourning and weeping in this vale of tears.

Turn, then, most gracious advocate, thine eyes of mercy toward us, and after this our exile show unto us the blessed fruit of thy womb, Jesus. O clement, O loving, O sweet Virgin Mary.

O Sacred Heart of Jesus, have mercy on us;
    O Mary, Queen of Peace, pray for us.
    In the name of the Father, the Son and the Holy Spirit. Amen.

❧

Please note that the meditations the Blessed Mother has given me for this special set of morning prayers cover every aspect of prayer and protection. Taken as a whole, these are very forceful prayers!

However, of course, Our Lady does not stop with her gifts of grace. She works tirelessly to help us to help ourselves through the Holy Spirit's power by constantly adding to our prayer life. Perhaps she best sums it up with this monthly message given on July 25, 1997: *"Dear children! Today I invite you to respond to my call to prayer. I desire, dear children, that during this time you find a corner for personal prayer. I desire to lea you towards prayer with the heart. Only in this way will you comprehend that your life is empty without prayer. You will discover the meaning of your life when you discover God in prayer. That is why, little children, open the door of your heart and you will comprehend that prayer is joy without which you cannot live. Thank you for having responded to my call."*

With the loving words of these morning prayers and the forthrightness of the above message in mind, let us explore another time of prayer Mary especially desires of us—prayer in the very early morning hours.

ELEVEN

In the Earliest Hours . . .

"Dear children! Today, again, I invite you to pray, so that through prayer, fasting, and small sacrifices you may prepare yourselves for the coming of Jesus. May this time, little children, be a time of grace for you. Use every moment and do good, for only in this way will you feel the birth of Jesus in your hearts. If with your life you give an example and become a sign of God's love, joy will prevail in the hearts of men. Thank you for having responded to my call."

(Message given November 25, 1996)

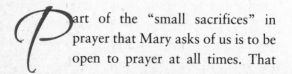 art of the "small sacrifices" in prayer that Mary asks of us is to be open to prayer at all times. That

includes the earliest morning hours, a "special penance of love" she asks of many souls.

I am one of those souls, and I have discovered that there are thousands more who have been called to do the same. We share an awakening in the wee hours, for many between three and four o'clock. We know in our hearts that we are being asked to accept the penance of love and to pray, especially for the conversion of souls, at this hour.

We literally pray with Gospa of Medjugorje at this early hour, who tells us through the visionaries that she prays at four o'clock every morning at the foot of the thirty-six-foot-high cement cross on Mount Krizevic, which overlooks the community of Medjugorje. Here is what she said in December 1981, when Ivan asked if it was really she appearing at the foot of the cross, as reported by several villagers: *"Yes, it is true. Almost every day I am at the foot of the cross. My Son carried the cross. He has suffered on the cross, and by it, he saved the world. Everyday I pray to my Son to forgive the sins of the world."*

The prayers given to me to be prayed at this hour are not necessarily the same as those given to others, but the intent is the same: to pray with Mary for the conversion of souls, and for peace in our world, which comes through the prayers of individuals.

Here are the prayers I pray at this hour, truly the beginning of my day of prayer:

All praise, glory, and honor to the Lord Jesus Christ.

🌱

Eternal Father, send down Your Holy Spirit and fill my heart and soul. Come, Holy Spirit, through the Immaculate Heart of the Blessed Virgin Mary, Your beloved Spouse. Amen.

🌱

My Holy Queen and Mother, I give myself entirely to you this day and every day, and to show you my love and devotion, I give to you my eyes, my ears, my heart, my everything.

Therefore, dear Mother, keep me and protect me as your property and your possession. Amen.

🌱

O my God, that You would bless me indeed and increase my territory. And that Your hand would guide me and keep me from evil, that I may not cause pain. Amen. (Based on the prayer of the prophet Jabez, found in the Old Testament at 1 Chronicles 4:10.)

My guardian angel, my guardian dear, to whom God's love commits me here, ever this day be at my side, to light and guard, to rule and guide. Amen.

If you wish to pray at this hour, your prayers may be the same as mine; that is, you can use these prayers, or you may pray those special prayers you feel you are asked to pray, or you may choose others. The point is to give a gift of penance by praying at this early hour. Some people feel they are asked to pray a full Rosary or a special litany at this time. There are thousands of recorded prayers that may be used, but the best, I think, is when you pray to the Holy Spirit to give you the prayers He wants you to pray at this hour.

Now, let's look at another prayer closely associated with Medjugorje. . . .

TWELVE

The Divine Mercy Chaplet

"Dear children, today I want to call all of you to decide for Paradise. The way is difficult for those who have not decided for God. Dear children, decide and believe that God is offering Himself to you in His fullness. You are invited and you need to answer the call of the Father, who is calling you through me. Pray, because in prayer each one of you will be able to achieve complete love. I am blessing you and I desire to help you so that each one of you might be under my motherly mantle. Thank you for having responded to my call."

(Monthly message given October 25, 1987)

In June 1986, I was on my second trip to Medjugorje in as many months. The trouble was, there weren't any other English-speaking pilgrims there at that time. After twelve days in Medjugorje with no one to really speak with, I was overjoyed when an American group arrived from Boston. It was the same organization with whom I had made my first trip to Medjugorje, the Center for Peace, led by Sister Margaret Catherine Sims. It was so good to see her and the group as they arrived at their hotel in Citluk, a short three miles from the village.

The following day as several of us walked the grounds in the afternoon, one of the group leaders, a vibrant, cheerful woman named Rose Finnigan, suddenly stopped and exclaimed, "O wow! It's three o'clock and time to pray the Divine Mercy Chaplet."

I look at her puzzled, still the Protestant so new to all of this business of praying this or that special prayer. "What is the Divine Mercy Chaplet?" I asked.

Excited to have the opportunity to introduce the prayer chaplet to someone, she began to tell me and several others in the group about a nun named Sister Faustina who had received the prayers straight from Jesus.

Hmm, I thought, maybe this is just a little bit far out. But as Rose explained the prayer and then led me and several others through it, I felt again that sensation within that Our Lady wanted me to learn this prayer and make it part of my developing daily prayer life.

Several years later, with the Divine Mercy Chaplet now well entrenched in my prayer life, I was in Poland on a speaking tour. It was shortly after the amazing and quick fall of Communism. Walking around the city of Crakow, I spotted a church and decided to enter it for a few minutes of prayer. As I walked into the church, which I was surprised to find filled with people in the middle of the afternoon, there was a sudden eruption as almost everyone at once got up from the pews and prostrated on the cold, stone floor. At first I did not realize what was happening. But then I remembered it was three o'clock, the time for the Divine Mercy Chaplet!

Later in the tour, I visited the tiny chapel where Sister Faustina had received the Chaplet. Now she lay entombed in one of the walls. I knelt next to her tomb and prayed the Divine Mercy Chaplet with many nuns present, dressed in the traditional and original habit as worn by Sister Faustina.

The Divine Mercy Chaplet is today a strongly integrated part of the Medjugorje experience, as well as a highly popular and still-spreading prayer of the church faithful. Divine Mercy images of Jesus adorn the walls of hundreds of churches. Of course, Sister Faustina is today St. Faustina. I highly recommend this prayer chaplet as part of your daily prayer life.

From a small booklet Rose gave the others and me when I first learned of the Divine Mercy Chaplet prayers, I discovered that Sister Faustina had a vision in 1935 of an angel sent by God to chastise a certain city. She began to pray for mercy, but her prayers seemed powerless. Suddenly she saw the Holy Trinity and felt the power of Jesus' grace within her. She began pleading with God for mercy with words she heard interiorly:

> Eternal Father, I offer You the body, blood, soul, and divinity of Your dearly beloved Son, Our Lord Jesus Christ, in atonement for our sins and those of the whole world. For the sake of His sorrowful passion, have mercy on us.

As she continued saying this inspired prayer, the angel became helpless and could not carry out the deserved punishment. The next day, as she was entering the chapel, she again heard this interior voice, instructing her how to recite the prayer that our Lord later called "the Chaplet." This time, after "have mercy on us," the words "and on the whole world" were added. From then on, she recited this form of prayer almost constantly, offering it especially for the dying.

In subsequent revelations, the Lord made it clear that the Chaplet was not just for her, but also for the whole world. He also attached extraordinary promises to its recitation, telling her, "Encourage souls to say the Chaplet which I have given you. Whoever will recite it will receive great mercy at the hour of death. When they say this Chaplet in the presence of the dying, I will stand between My Father and the dying person, not as the just Judge but as the Merciful Savior. Priests will recommend it to sinners as their last hope of salvation. Even if there were a sinner most hardened, if he were to recite this Chaplet only once, he would receive grace from My infinite mercy. I desire to grant unimaginable graces to those souls who trust in My mercy. Through the Chaplet you will obtain everything, if what you ask for is compatible with My will."

So, there you have it: more than enough reason to make this powerful Divine Mercy Chaplet part of your daily prayer life. I begin my Rosary prayers with its pleading prayer of mercy and try to spread it to as many people as possible.

Those praying the Divine Mercy Chaplet use their rosary beads. Formerly, it was an intercessory prayer that extended the offering of the Eucharist, so it is especially appropriate to use it after having received Holy Communion at Holy Mass. One may say it at any time, but Jesus specifically told St. Faustina to recite it beginning on Good Friday for nine days, ending on the Sunday after Easter, known as the Feast of Mercy. He then added, "By this novena, I will grant every possible grace to souls." However, it is likewise appropriate—and most popular—to pray the Chaplet during the "Hour of Great Mercy"—three o'clock each afternoon (recalling the time of Christ's death on the cross). In His revelations to St. Faustina, our Lord asked for a special remembrance of His passion at that hour. This is my way of never forgetting the great mercy God has given us in the death of His Son on the cross.

The Divine Mercy Chaplet

WE BEGIN WITH THE OUR FATHER

Our Father, who is in heaven, hallowed be Your name. Your kingdom come, Your will be done, on earth as it is in heaven.

Give us this day our daily bread, and forgive us our trespasses as we forgive those who trespass against us; and lead us not into temptation, but deliver us from evil. Amen.

NEXT IS THE HAIL MARY

Hail Mary, full of grace, the Lord is with you. Blessed are you among women, and blessed is the fruit of your womb, Jesus.

Holy Mary, Mother of God, pray for us sinners, now and at the hour of our death. Amen.

NOW THE CREED

I believe in God, the Father Almighty, Creator of heaven and earth, and in Jesus Christ, His only Son, our Lord, who was conceived by the Holy Spirit, born of the Virgin Mary, suffered under Pontius Pilate, was crucified, died, and was buried. He descended into hell. The third day He arose again from the dead. He ascended into heaven and is seated at the right hand of the Father.

From thence He shall come to judge the living and the dead.

I believe in the Holy Spirit, the holy catholic church, the communion of saints, the forgiveness of sins, the resurrection of the body, and the life everlasting. Amen.

THE FIRST DECADE
(prayed on the rosary beads):

I pray this decade in remembrance of the wound in the right hand of Jesus.

Eternal Father, I offer You the body, blood, soul, and divinity of our dearly beloved Lord Jesus Christ, in atonement for our sins and those of the whole world. For the sake of His sorrowful passion, have mercy on us and on the whole world. (To be said ten times.)

THE SECOND DECADE

I pray this decade in remembrance of the wound in the left hand of Jesus.

ETERNAL FATHER 10X

THE THIRD DECADE

I pray this decade in remembrance of the wound in the right foot of Jesus.

ETERNAL FATHER 10X

THE FOURTH DECADE

I pray this decade in remembrance of the wound in the left foot of Jesus.

ETERNAL FATHER 10X

THE FIFTH DECADE

I pray this decade in remembrance of the wound in the side of Jesus. Pour forth Your blood and water to wash away our sins, Lord Jesus, and those of the entire world.

ETERNAL FATHER 10X

We then pray three times:

Holy God, holy mighty One, holy immortal One, have mercy on us and on the whole world.

We end the Chaplet by praying three times:

Jesus, I trust in You!

❧

The graces received for praying this beautiful Chaplet given to St. Faustina are endless. Again, we can pray it at any time, including during a wondrous time of intimacy with Jesus: adoration.

We now look at Adoration of Jesus in the Blessed Sacrament of the Altar as they pray it in Medjugorje. . . .

THIRTEEN

I Adore You, Jesus!

"Dear children, today I invite you to fall in love with the most Holy Sacrament of the Altar. Adore Him, little children in your parishes, and in this way you will be united with the entire world. Jesus will become your friend and you will not talk of Him like someone whom you barely know. Unity with Him will be a joy for you and you will become witnesses to the love of Jesus that He has for every creature. When you adore Jesus, you are also close to me. Thank you for your response to my call."

(Message given on September 25, 1995)

Let me say from the outset of this chapter that there is nothing quite as sweet as Adoration of the Blessed Sacrament of the Altar in Medjugorje!

This is the intimacy, the personal touch, the pure love of conversation with God that I have mentioned so many times up to this point. All of the prayers discussed and recorded up to now can and are used in adoration. However, Our Lady says it best in the message above, that this is a time to adore our Jesus and to speak to Him with abandonment in praise and thanksgiving.

Can you imagine anywhere from 500 to more than 5,000 pilgrims and villagers gathered together late at night in St. James Church, or outside behind the church at the outdoor altar, all singing and praying directly to Jesus in many different languages? Can you mentally picture thousands of young people participating, as happens annually at the Youth Festival in the first week of August? Regardless of the weather, it occurs in Medjugorje two or more times weekly.

There is always an overall hush among the crowd during Adoration of the Blessed Sacrament, interrupted only by a quiet voice leading the prayers in the different languages. Songs of worship are interspersed among the periods of silent contemplation and the utterances of intimate prayers. Remarkably, there is not even the sound of coughing or other inevitable human noise expected from large crowds. This becomes a time of pure, sincere adoration of Jesus in the Holy Sacrament of the Altar.

Each of us must personalize our prayers and be specific with our intentions. I do this most of all during moments of sincere adoration.

There is not a long list of specific prayers other than those already recorded (the Holy Rosary, Divine Mercy, prayers to the Holy Spirit) that I wish to list here. Rather, I will give you a "sample" of short utterances that have been prayed in Medjugorje during adoration. You may want to pray these words; but also, be inspired to personalize your prayers in your own, God-inspired ways!

Dear Jesus, I love You unconditionally. I come before You in joy that You are here and so real in the Blessed Sacrament.

Jesus, help me to pray for those who do not love me; help me to forgive as You forgive.

Lord, fill my heart with Your presence; I want to belong to You, Jesus. I want to do

Your will.
Heal my heart, Jesus.

Heal my body, Jesus.

Dear Jesus, I want to be Your instrument of
peace, to bring peace to those in my family
and in my workplace and in my school.

Adoration is a time to simply allow what is
in your heart to flow out in words, in silence,
and in song. It took me a while to learn how
to do this, how to just let it happen. Finally, I
realized that all I had to do was open up my
heart, just as Jesus opens up His heart for us.
As usual, this happened without warning. I
was on a speaking tour in England, and we
were having an all-day Saturday conference in
Manchester. Tony Hickey, my host for the
tour, had been having these special confer-
ences for several years. Those attending were
mostly Medjugorje converts and followers,
and the time of the conference was a time of
renewal through prayer, just as they had
learned it in Medjugorje.

That afternoon, we were having Adoration
of Jesus in the Blessed Sacrament of the Altar.
Just before we were to begin, Tony asked if I

would lead the prayers. I was a bit taken aback because it was something he normally did, but I agreed. "What do you want to pray?" I asked Tony, "the Rosary, or what?"

Tony looked at me and in a quiet voice said, "No, not the Rosary, just whatever comes to you."

I gulped. "Yeah, okay, but for how long?"

"Well, adoration is an hour."

My heart leaped. "You want me to pray for an hour? With just whatever comes to mind?" I was near panic, as we were scheduled to begin in just a matter of minutes. There was no time to plan or prepare other than just doing it!

Tony smiled softly and said with a little pat, "You can do it."

And I did. The panic left after the first fifteen minutes. I was in freefall! The words just came, and at no time did I need to pause and think of what to say. I experienced the pure holy power from the Holy Spirit.

This experience of Adoration of Jesus in the Blessed Sacrament was the beginning of many such hours of adoration, some in public like this one and others when I was all by myself.

You can do the same kind of impromptu freefall of prayer. Just let go and let God when you pray. . . .

FOURTEEN

Her Special Motherly Blessing

"*Dear children, today I am grateful to you for your presence in this place, where I am giving you special graces. I call each one of you to begin to live as of today that life which God wishes of you and to begin to perform good works of love and mercy. I do not want you, dear children, to live the message and be committing sin which is displeasing to me. Therefore, dear children, I want each of you to live a new life without the murder of all that God produces in you and is giving you. I give you my* special blessing (emphasis added) *and I am remaining with you on your way to conversion. Thank you for having responded to my call.*"

(Monthly message given March 25, 1987)

*T*alk about graces!

Our Lady has obtained for us a powerful grace that we can use for healing our families and friends and others of spiritual and physical ailments. She has passed on to us a special grace directly from her spouse, the Holy Spirit. She obtained this grace from Him and gives it to us, asking us to put it to use. God wants us to be part of His plan of salvation for the entire world!

This special grace is a prayer, a communication with God, a request to bring healing and help to those to whom we give it. She asked me to use this special prayer almost from the beginning of my mission.

Let us look once again in the messages Mary has imparted to the visionaries of Medjugorje in order to see the origins of this special prayer. The earliest message mentioning a special blessing from Our Lady was March 25, 1987, listed at the beginning of this chapter, where she starts by reminding us that she giving us *"special graces."* She then calls on us to *"begin to perform good works of love and mercy."* Later, she solidifies it by stating: *"I give you*

*my special blessing, and I am remaining
with you on your way to conversion."*

Sometime in March of 1987, I began to feel
in my heart that *I was to give this special
blessing* from her to all of the people who
came to my talks on Medjugorje. Of course, I
was to personally give the blessing to my own
family and friends, and even to strangers. On
every occasion from that point on, when I
would see an ambulance or police car or a
wreck or someone going through crisis, I
would give them "Mary's Special Motherly
Blessing." You can, too.

In November 1988, I flew to Birmingham,
Alabama, to visit with the visionary Marija,
who was there to give her kidney to her
brother Andrija. He was terminally ill with a
kidney disease. Here was a visionary doing
exactly what Jesus would have her do: helping
her brother by giving a part of herself. This
sacrifice was a dramatic fulfillment of her
messages over the previous seven years
of apparitions.

Thanks to Terry Colafrancesco, founder of an
organization called Caritas of Birmingham,
arrangements were hastily made to bring Marija
and Andrija to the University of Alabama at

Birmingham, one of the leading medical centers for treatment of kidney disease and transplants. While there, Marija received this special message from Our Lady on November 29: *"Dear children: Bless even those who don't believe. You can give them this blessing from the heart to help them in their conversion. Bless everyone you meet. I gave you a special grace. I want you to give this grace to others."*

Could this gift of grace from the Blessed Mother be any clearer or greater? She had also mentioned it in the monthly message to Marija on the 25th: *"Dear children, I am calling you to peace. Live peace in your heart and in your surroundings, so that all may recognize the peace, which does not come from you, but from God. Little children, today is a great day. Rejoice with me! Celebrate the birth of Jesus with my peace, the peace with which I came as your Mother, Queen of Peace. Today I am giving you my special blessing. Carry it to every creature so that each one may have peace. Thank you for having responded to my call."*

I was graced to be with Marija when she received the two messages above about the special blessing. My presence there at that time was no coincidence, I discerned later. Our Lady wanted me to give the blessing to everyone in the audience every time I gave a talk on Medjugorje. The objective was to assure those in the audience that they were to be part of God's plan of salvation by giving this blessing to those put in their pathway.

Further confirmation came in the monthly message on January 25, 1989: *"Dear children, today I am calling you to the way of holiness. Pray that you may comprehend the beauty and the greatness of this way, where God reveals Himself to you in a special way. Pray that you may be open to everything that God is doing through you, and that in your life you may be enabled to give thanks to God and to rejoice over everything that He is doing through each individual. I am giving you my* Blessing (emphasis added). *Thank you for having responded to my call."*

Again, on the anniversary of the apparitions, June 25, 1989, Mary repeated the gift of a special blessing: *"Dear children, today I call you to live the messages which I have been giving you during the past eight years. This is a time of graces and I desire that the grace of God be great for every single one of you. I am blessing you and I love you with a special love. Thank you for having responded to my call"* (emphasis added).

So here it is: a direct, personal request from Mary for us, her spiritual children, to accept and to use holy power to help our brothers and sisters in Christ. As always, it is an informal, personal prayer with words that we can use in different ways and at different times. For example, you can say, "I give you Mary's special blessing"; or, "I give you Our Lady's special motherly blessing." I'm sure you get the idea. She tells us to use it often, especially on those people in our lives as well as strangers in need, and to "bombard" the recipient with grace!

While on a speaking tour in South Africa several years ago, I gave the blessing to an audience as I usually do after the talk. However, I felt Mary's presence in my heart, asking something new: She wanted me to tell the people to use this newly given grace *right then and there!* I told them, "Our Lady is asking you to use the special blessing right now for that one person or persons in your heart that you know needs it the most." By the looks on the faces of those in the audience, I knew that this was a much-needed addition to the special blessing.

Several nights later after the talk, people came up to me and stated that they had been there that evening when I gave the special blessing and asked them to use it then. The stories were astonishing! One woman told me of giving the blessing to her son who had fallen away from the church and was into all the wrong things. "It was so unbelievable," she said, as the tears began, "I gave him the blessing and when I arrived home and walked into the door, my son met me and hugged me and said, 'Mom, I really need to get back to church with you and start living right.'" She then hugged me and thanked me for telling them about the blessing and the need to use it immediately.

You know, if you really believe in this holy power that fuels prayer, you know that it works for huge things, such as the story above, but also for little things. The next story I heard about using the blessing that night confirmed it. A second woman came up to me and said, "Maybe this is a bit ridiculous, but I gave that special blessing to a police officer who gave me a speeding ticket! I really didn't think I was speeding and have been very upset over it."

I laughed and told her that that was okay, because the graces of heaven are for little things also. "Yes, but listen to this," she continued, "I went to the station to pay the ticket, accepting the fact that I needed to get over it and have my peace again." She paused for effect. "They couldn't find a record of the ticket, so I didn't have to pay anything!"

May I suggest this little prayer for using this phenomenal grace of Our Lady's special blessing? Begin with:

Dearest Mother of God, I give your special motherly blessing to _____ (list the person). Please, may this blessing bring healing and true peace now and forever. Amen.

Have faith that Mary is pleased each and every time you use this grace she has obtained for you.

FIFTEEN

Holy Mass Prayers

"Dear children, God wants to make you holy. Therefore, through me He is calling you to complete surrender. Let the Holy Mass be your life. Understand that the church is God's palace, the place in which I gather you and want to show you the way of God. Come and pray! Neither look to others nor slander them, but rather let your life be a testimony on the way of holiness. Churches deserve respect and are set apart as holy because God, Who became Man, dwells in them day and night. Therefore, little children, believe and pray that the Father increases your faith, and then ask for whatever you need. I am with you and I rejoice because of your conversion and I am protecting you with my motherly mantle. Thank you for having responded to my call."

(Monthly message given April 25, 1988)

*I*n the early days of the apparitions of the Blessed Mother in Medjugorje, she made clear to the visionaries the place of Holy Mass in their lives: *"The Mass is the greatest prayer of God. You will never be able to understand its greatness. That is why you must be perfect and humble at Mass, and you should prepare yourselves there."*

There is no greater "prayer" than the Holy Mass. As Our Lady states in the opening message above, the church is God's palace. His house is a place to converse with His creation in deep, contemplative, yet intimate conversation. We literally commune with God and receive Holy Spirit grace directly at the Holy Mass.

I find the church to be the holiest place of prayer and the most opportune time to focus our desire for answers to our prayer requests. We are to be attentive children, participating in every way we can.

On April 21, 1983, Mary spoke to the visionaries—especially Jakov—concerning behavior during Mass and around others: *"You must behave well; be pious and set a good example for the faithful."* On other occasions she chastised the visionary Marija for not focusing on the grace of the Holy Mass, for chatting too much to others around her. Constantly, she pointed out to all of them the need to be completely *involved* during the liturgy. Our involvement begins the moment we enter the doors of the church.

Sadly, the chastisement from Mary concerning behavior at Mass should extend beyond the young people to many adults today. Why is it that so many turn this time of ultimate prayer into just another social event? We talk, laugh, and wave to one another; all good things, but better done outside of the church and after the Mass.

Listen to the teachings about the Mass Our Lady gave the parish of St. James in Medjugorje during her weekly Thursday messages: *"Today, I call you to renew prayer in your families. Dear children, encourage the very young to pray and the children to go to Holy Mass* . . . (March 7, 1985); *. . . I am calling you to a more active prayer and attendance at Holy Mass. I wish your Mass to be an experience of God"* (May 16, 1985).

With this motherly admonishment, let us consider how to open our hearts to the Mass and how to pray during the liturgy. Again, these are special prayers I feel Mary has given me to use at specific times during the service. There are not many, and that is because the entire Mass is prayer.

My prayer with the blessing of holy water is this:

Cleanse and purify me, O Lord, that I might receive Jesus in the Holy Eucharist with a pure heart and soul.

As always throughout the pages of this book, I remind you that you can use this prayer or create your own. Remember, it is *your* personal time with God, and you can express it in a way to reinforce that bond of intimacy.

Now, as we enter and take a seat, our hearts are ready to spend quiet time contemplating the greatest of all miracles of heaven: the Holy Eucharist. Listen to this: the miracle of the Eucharist makes the miracle of apparitions— including Medjugorje—pale in comparison! Jesus comes to us as *true flesh* and *true blood*. He willingly enters into us to become part of us, and we become part of Him. We are then asked to take Him into our daily lives, into the world, and to do what He would do with every penance and opportunity to serve, that crosses our paths. I am in awe of this greatest of all miracles before every Holy Mass.

As the liturgy begins and we sign ourselves with the sign of the cross, my prayer is:

Lord, I mark myself with the sign of Your redemptive gift to us, Your death on the cross, so that we might have life eternal.

The next part of the liturgy, the prayer for forgiveness, should be a time to search our souls to assure that all possible venial sins to be forgiven are in the forefront of our mind:

I confess to Almighty God, and to you, my brothers and sisters, that I have sinned in my thoughts and in my words; in what I have done and in what I have failed to do; and I ask Blessed Mary and all her angels and saints to pray for me to the Lord our God.

I include this prayer said in the Holy Mass to underscore the importance of public confession, but also *private* confession with a priest to clean out all sins before receiving the miracle of the Eucharist. Such actions are acts of love on our part. Do we want to purposely offend Jesus, who gave the ultimate in sacrifice for each one of us on the cross? For this reason alone we should exercise the sacrament of confession at least once a month, as our Blessed Mother asks of us in her messages.

So many people take the Holy Eucharist for granted or do not comprehend its full meaning. They seem unaware of its unlimited grace. Our Lady calls us to the Holy Mass with this thought in mind. That is why it is the *"greatest prayer of God."* That is why she continues to appear in apparition in Medjugorje, so that all possible souls will awaken from the slumber of "obligation" attendance at Holy Mass to full and willing participation.

Now, for the most powerful time for prayers during the Mass: the consecration of the gifts. When the priest lifts the host and consecrates it, I pray:

Lord, I offer Your holy body for all victim souls, especially those of abortion, war, terrorism, and broken families.

When the priest lifts the precious blood, I pray:

Lord, I pray especially for all of the souls of purgatory to enter into heaven.
I pray for the Holy Father, Pope Benedict XVI, and all priests of the church.
I pray in thanksgiving for allowing the Blessed Virgin Mary to walk the earth in apparition, especially in Medjugorje.

As we receive Jesus in the Holy Eucharist, we experience the highlight, the purpose, the *everything* of the Holy Mass. My prayer before receiving is the Stella Maris, which I learned from the *Pieta Prayer Book*. Why Our Lady chose this for me to pray at this time I can only find in the words:

Hail, thou star of ocean, portal of the sky, ever-virgin mother of the Lord most high.
O! by Gabriel's "Ave," uttered long ago, Eva's name reversing, established peace below;
Break the captive's fetters, light on blindness pour, all our ills expelling, every bliss implore.
Show thyself a mother, offer Him our sighs, who for us incarnate, did not thee despise.

Virgin of all virgins, to thy shelter take us. Gentlest of the gentle, chaste and gentle make us;
Still, as on we journey, help our weak endeavor, till with thee and Jesus, we rejoice forever.
Through the highest heaven, to the Almighty Three: Father, Son, and Spirit, one same glory be.

In the tenth century, an unknown author composed this beautiful anthem that is usually sung at vespers on most feasts of Mary. The words have been modernized, but the power and awe remain as in the original.

For me, it is a thank you to Our Lady. Without her, I would not know of Jesus in the Holy Eucharist; I would not be present at the Mass celebration and be a participant with millions in the greatest of all miracles, the receiving of the body and blood of our Lord.

We now embark on our final course of study in the School of Prayer as we look at other prayers that have become part of the apparitions of Mary at Medjugorje . . .

SIXTEEN

Short and Ardent Prayers of Medjugorje

*"Dear children! Also today, I call you to fill your day with **short and ardent prayers** (emphasis added). When you pray, your heart is open, and God loves you with a special love and gives you special graces. Therefore, make good use of this time of grace and devote it to God more than ever up to now. Do novenas of fasting and renunciation so that Satan be far from you and grace be around you. I am near you and intercede before God for each of you. Thank you for having responded to my call."*

(Monthly message given July 25, 2005)

Thus far, we have discussed and studied many of the special prayers Mary has given us or asked of us through her messages in Medjugorje. Some are longer, formal prayers and others are those very *"short and ardent prayers"* she asks for in the monthly message of July 2005. Mary has inspired me with many short and ardent prayers over the years. On one occasion, while driving, I was so struck by grace that I pulled the car to the side of the road, unable to drive safely because tears of joy filled my eyes. I kept saying, "I love you, Mary! I love you, Jesus!" These were my first short and ardent prayers.

The visionary Marija told me that after each apparition experience, once Our Lady vanishes in the same light in which she arrives, she is requested to pray the Magnificat. That glorious prayer is an excellent example of a short and ardent prayer, and one that Mary loves; thus, it would be good to include this prayer at some point in your day:

My being proclaims the greatness of the Lord; my spirit finds joy in God my savior, for He has looked upon His servant in her lowliness; all ages to come shall call me blessed. God, who is mighty, has done great things for me; holy is His name. His mercy is from age to age on those who

fear Him. He has shown might with His arm. He has confused the proud in their inmost thoughts. He has deposed the mighty from their thrones and raised the lowly to high places. The hungry He has given every good thing, while the rich He has sent empty away. He has upheld Israel His servant, ever mindful of His mercy, even as He promised our fathers, Abraham and His descendants forever.
(Luke 1:46–55)

Another popular prayer with followers of Medjugorje is the Angelus, because it is often prayed by the villagers:

℣: The angel of the Lord declared unto Mary
℟ : *And she conceived by the Holy Ghost.*
℣: Hail Mary, full of grace: the Lord is with thee. Blessed art thou among women, and blessed is the fruit of thy womb, Jesus.
℟: *Holy Mary, Mother of God: Pray for us sinners, now and at the hour of our death. Amen.*
℣: Behold the handmaid of the Lord.
℟ : *Be it done unto me according to thy word.*
℣: Hail Mary. . . .

℞ : *Holy Mary.* . . .
℣: And the Word was made flesh
℞ : *And dwelt among us.*
℣: Hail Mary. . . .
℞ : *Holy Mary.* . . .
℣: Pray for us, O holy Mother of God,
℞ : *That we may be made worthy of the promises of Christ.*
℞ : Let us pray.

Pour forth, we beseech thee, O Lord, thy grace unto our hearts, that we, to whom the incarnation of Christ, thy Son, was made known by the message of an angel, may by His passion and cross be brought to the glory of His resurrection, through the same Christ, our Lord. Amen.

This next prayer is probably my favorite short and ardent prayer. You may say it at any time of the day or night. I usually pray these words after my Rosary prayers, but many times just while driving, playing golf, or whatever. I pray three times:

O my God, I believe, I adore, I hope, and I love You. I pray pardon for those who do not believe, do not adore, do not hope, and do not love You.

Of course, there are many more short prayers I could list here, but you get the idea. Either add your own from memory, or create them out of love and thanksgiving. I highly recommend the fifteen St. Brigitte prayers, which can be found in the popular *Pieta Prayer Book*. They are not short and ardent, but long and intense. Our Lord's request is that we pray them daily for an entire year to learn a deep appreciation of His holy passion.

Lastly, we have wonderful, holy songs, an incredible cache of prayer. All songs relating to our faith are prayer and are usually prayers of joy. On November 3, 1981, Mary demonstrated her own love for song when she began singing to the visionaries at Medjugorje, *"Come, come to us, Lord."* The visionaries then joined in. That first occasion would later be followed by others when the Blessed Mother would sing with them or recommend hymns to them.

One song that is very special to me is "Here I am, Lord." The following verse serves as my personal "theme song" for my life spent fulfilling what Mary asks of me:

Here I am, Lord.
Is it I, Lord?

I have heard you calling in the night.
I will go, Lord.
If you lead me;
I will hold your people in my heart.

Finally, the last prayer I share with you is, again, one that I feel Mary has given me and asked me to end my day with:

O God, I offer you the Sacred Heart of Jesus, with all of its love, suffering, and merit.
Glory be to the Father, Son, and Holy Spirit; as it was in the beginning, is now, and ever shall be, world without end.
To purify the good I have done badly this day and each day of my life.
Glory be. . . .
And to supply the good I should have done but have failed to do this day and each day of my life.
Glory be. . . .
I love you, Jesus;
I love you, Mary.
Give me rest, O Holy Spirit of God.
Amen.

❧

So there you are: *The Medjugorje Prayer Book*, which I pray you will use daily and frequently. You are now ready to graduate from Our Lady's special Medjugorje School of Prayer . . .

SEVENTEEN

Graduation from the School of Prayer

"Dear children! Also today I call you to renew prayer in your families. By prayer and the reading of sacred scripture, may the Holy Spirit, who will renew you, enter into your families. In this way, you will become teachers of the faith (emphasis added) *in your family. By prayer and your love, the world will set out on a better way and love will begin to rule in the world. Thank you for having responded to my call."*

(Monthly message given April 25, 2005)

As a graduate of the Medjugorje School of Prayer, you are now a teacher of the school as well. Mary is asking each of us to become ambassadors of prayer, starting within our families. She asks us to commit ourselves to prayer, and specifically to become part of a prayer group. We then extend the "family" by including all of our brothers and sisters in Christ. These groups can and should include people of all faiths.

Make no mistake about her intent in the above message: we are to be teachers for our family by example and by gathering our children together regardless of worldly schedules. Family prayer is necessary if we truly are to bring the peace of Christ to earth. Group prayer, the extended family, does the same.

The guest speaker at your graduation ceremony is the teacher who has led you to this point, Our Lady. Her speech to you is like all of her previous teachings and lectures through her messages—short and sweet and to the point:

"Tell all my sons and daughters, tell all the world as soon as possible that I desire their conversion. The only word I tell the world is, convert and do not delay. I will ask my Son not to punish the world but that the world be saved. You do not, and cannot, know what God will send to the world. Convert, renounce everything, be ready for everything, because all this is part of the conversion."

I hope you make good use of all of the prayers contained in this prayer book. You may add to them with your own favorites. The theme that gives character to all the prayers gleaned from the wondrous apparitions in Medjugorje is the personal, intimate presence of Mary, mother of Jesus, spiritual mother of each one of us. Please remember this when you pray. Ask her to intercede, to give you her own personal touch to your prayers.

May the peace, the grace, and the love of Jesus be with you!

ABOUT PARACLETE PRESS

Paraclete Press is an ecumenical publisher of books and recordings on Christian spirituality. Our publishing represents a full expression of Christian belief and practice—from Catholic to Evangelical, from Protestant to Orthodox.

Paraclete Press is the publishing arm of the Community of Jesus, an ecumenical monastic community in the Benedictine tradition. As such, we are uniquely positioned in the marketplace without connection to a large corporation and with informal relationships to many branches and denominations of faith.

We like it best when people buy our books from booksellers, our partners in successfully reaching as wide an audience as possible.

Books

Paraclete Press publishes books that show the richness and depth of what it means to be Christian. Although Benedictine spirituality is at the heart of all that we do, we publish books that reflect the Christian experience across many cultures, time periods, and houses of worship.

We publish books that nourish the vibrant life of the church and its people—books about spiritual practice, formation, history, ideas, and customs.

We have several different series of books within Paraclete Press, including the best-selling Living Library series of modernized classic texts; A Voice from the Monastery—giving voice to men and women monastics about what it means to live a spiritual life today; award-winning literary faith fiction; and books that explore Judaism and Islam and discover how these faiths inform Christian thought and practice.

Recordings

From Gregorian chant to contemporary American choral works, our music recordings celebrate the richness of sacred choral music through the centuries. Paraclete is proud to distribute the recordings of the internationally acclaimed choir Gloriæ Dei Cantores, who have been praised for their "rapt and fathomless spiritual intensity" by *American Record Guide*, and the Gloriæ Dei Cantores Schola, which specializes in the study and performance of Gregorian chant. Paraclete is also the exclusive North American distributor of the recordings of the Monastic Choir of St. Peter's Abbey in Solesmes, France, long considered to be a leading authority on Gregorian chant performance.